BY THE FIRE

By the Fire

SAMI FOLKTALES *and* LEGENDS

Collected and Illustrated by
EMILIE DEMANT HATT

Translated by Barbara Sjoholm

University of Minnesota Press
Minneapolis
London

Frontispiece: Emilie Demant Hatt, "The Sami lad and his Halde wife then moved up to the high mountains with their reindeer," linocut print, circa 1922.

DANISH ARTS FOUNDATION

The University of Minnesota Press gratefully acknowledges the generous assistance provided for the publication of this book from the Danish Arts Foundation.

Originally published in Danish as *Ved ilden. Eventyr og historier fra Lapland* (Copenhagen: J. H. Schultz Forlag, 1922).

Translation and Afterword copyright 2019 by Barbara Sjoholm

Published by the University of Minnesota Press
111 Third Avenue South, Suite 290
Minneapolis, MN 55401-2520
http://www.upress.umn.edu

Printed in the United States of America on acid-free paper

The University of Minnesota is an equal-opportunity educator and employer.

27 26 25 24 23 22   10 9 8 7 6 5 4 3 2 1

Library of Congress Cataloging-in-Publication Data
Demant Hatt, Emilie, 1873-1958, compiler and illustrator. | Sjoholm, Barbara, translator.
By the fire : Sami folktales and legends / collected and illustrated by Emilie Demant Hatt ;
    translated by Barbara Sjoholm.
Other titles: Ved ilden. English
Minneapolis : University of Minnesota Press, 2019. | Includes bibliographical references. |
Identifiers: LCCN 2018024549 (print) | ISBN 978-1-5179-0457-9 (hc) |
    ISBN 978-1-5179-0458-6 (pb)
Subjects: LCSH: Sami (European people)—Folklore. | Folklore—Lapland. |
    Legends—Lapland.
Classification: LCC GR138.5 .V3413 2019 (print) | DDC 398.2094897/7—dc23
LC record available at https://lccn.loc.gov/2018024549

Contents

———

Folktales   47

———

Russian Chudes and Other Enemies   69

Translator's Note

Almost as far back as the Danish artist and ethnographer Emilie Demant Hatt (1873–1958) could remember, tales of Sami reindeer nomads had gripped her imagination. Eventually, in 1904, Demant Hatt traveled with her sister as a tourist to northern Sweden. There, by chance, she met a man who became a close friend: the artist, writer, and hunter Johan Turi, who introduced her to his family and to the nomadic way of life. In 1907, after studying the Northern Sami language at the University of Copenhagen, Demant Hatt returned to the north of Sweden and lived for eighteen months among the nomadic herders, first with Johan Turi's brother Aslak and sister-in-law Siri and their children in a tent near Lake Torneträsk and then with the Rasti family of Karesuando, with whom she made the spring reindeer migration over the mountains to Norway. From her letters and notes, Demant Hatt wrote a lively narrative of travel and ethnography, *With the Lapps in the High Mountains* (1913). She also worked with Johan Turi on his collection of narratives, *Muitalus sámiid birra*, or *An Account of the Sámi* (1910), the first important long narrative to be written in Sami by a Sami author.

From 1910 through 1916, Demant Hatt traveled most summers in Sápmi, particularly in the mountain border districts of Sweden and Norway, to collect information on reindeer herding and domestic life from the Sami families she stayed with. Sleeping in tents and usually traveling by foot, Demant Hatt (on her own in 1910 and 1911 and then from 1912 to 1916 with her husband, Gudmund Hatt) filled field journals and sketchbooks with ethnographic observations, folklore, drawings, and watercolors. In 1922, now back in Denmark, Emilie retold some of the folktales and legends she had collected during her travels and published them in a book she titled *By the Fire*. She included around sixty-five shorter and longer narratives, accompanied by field notes on Sami folklore and examples of variants of some of the tales. She illustrated the book with twenty-four black-and-white linocuts, most of them influenced by Expressionist trends in European art. This collection, long out of print, is published here in its first English translation, along with her original art and a selection of photographs of the storytellers.

Because it fits in so well with the collection, I took the liberty of adding a narrative that was not in the original publication of *By the Fire* but was told by one of Demant Hatt's main storytellers, Märta Nilsson. "The Sami Girls Who Escaped the Bandits" is from an unpublished manuscript, "Long Ago," that Demant Hatt wrote in the 1940s about her stay with Märta and Nils Nilsson in Glen, Sweden, in the summer of 1910.

My more significant intervention lies in identifying many of the storytellers and placing their names at the end of individual folktales and legends. Although in her original notes to *By the Fire* Demant Hatt mentions only generally the Sami community or district where she recorded the tale, in her typed field journals she often adds the name of the narrator or narrators. I was not able to correlate every story and teller with complete certainty. In one instance, Demant Hatt wrote years later that all the stories from Jämtland in *By the Fire* came from Märta Nilsson of Glen, yet because Jämtland is a large region, it's certain that at least a few were told by other narrators. Likewise, most of the stories from Karesaundo were told by Anni or Jouna Rasti, but not all could be identified from Demant Hatt's field journals. Where I was unsure, only the geographic region is mentioned. The Afterword to this volume provides more historical and biographical background for the tales and their tellers, as well as commentary about the illustrations.

In translating the stories and the additional material written by Demant Hatt in the original edition, I've changed the older words Lapp or Lappish to Sami, which is both an adjective and a noun, singular and plural. (Thus, Sami can refer to the Sami people or to an individual, as well as to the Sami language. It is sometimes spelled Sámi or Saami.) In the early twentieth century, when Demant Hatt was living among and writing about the Sami, the use of the term Lapp was still common; it now has a primarily historic use. Demant Hatt herself began to use the word Sami in the 1940s when typing her field notes. I left her geographic term Lapmarks but usually changed Lapland to Sápmi.

The folktales and legends in *By the Fire* have been translated from Danish, but the original text includes many words and phrases in Sami, only some of which have been retained in this English edition. We can assume that Demant Hatt included such expressions because they conjured for her a real sense of the time and place where she collected the story; she did the same when writing *With the Lapps in the High Mountains*. In my translation of that book I chose to keep a number of Sami expressions and words to preserve something of the historic flavor of her travel narrative within a region where Northern Sami was the spoken language.

In translating *By the Fire* I have taken a different approach, because this collection is intended for readers who may be unfamiliar with Sami cultures and languages. Here I omitted most Sami sentences and several individual Sami words (many of which refer to objects connected to tent life and animals) and instead translated her Danish glosses of the Sami words. Thus, *ræppen* is "smoke hole" throughout, and *raggas* is a "mosquito tent." The Sami words I retained, such as *siida* and *joik*, often represent concepts larger than a single English word can suggest. They are defined in the text in passing, and more substantial definitions can be found in Demant Hatt's original notes, along with occasional additions from me if necessary, in "Field Notes and Commentary" after the folktales.

When it comes to proper names, especially for supernatural beings, I've taken a different tack and left them all, while following Demant Hatt's lead in defining them. She provides many fuller definitions or explanations in her notes. In the original Danish edition of *By the Fire*, Demant Hatt supplied a glossary of two dozen Sami words for things and animals as well as for proper names. Rather inconsistently, this glossary does not list all the Sami words in the stories, though it does include a few Swedish and Norwegian words. I jettisoned this glossary here but added a few of her definitions (including an entry on the joik) in brackets in the notes.

As Demant Hatt explains in her Introduction, she collected her material from various regions of Swedish Sápmi, where different languages were spoken. She devised (with the help of the professor of Finno-Ugric languages at Uppsala University, K. B. Wiklund) a kind of simplified orthography for the Sami words and expressions in her text, one that leaves off diacritical marks and case endings. The choice of how to spell the Sami words in the folktales was not always obvious. Many stories come from districts where Northern Sami was and is spoken, but just as many come from South Sápmi and from Pite Sápmi, the north-central region around Arjeplog where the Pite Sami language (now almost extinct) was spoken. Putting everything into the distinct orthography of Northern Sami did not seem appropriate; I decided instead to leave the spellings of all the proper nouns and names and many common words as they were. The Russian Tjsudes have become the more common Chudes (*Čuđit* in Northern Sami). Demant Hatt's rendering of *epper,* the dead-child spirit, has also been allowed to stand as she wrote it (the current Northern Sami spelling is *eahpáraš*). Demant Hatt's notes are often very useful guides to the meanings of words, though she would have been the first to say she was no trained linguist. We can enjoy her ability to convey in Danish a story she originally heard in one of the Sami languages or in a combination of a Sami language and Swedish.

My aim has been to present an English text that will honor both Demant's Danish and the Sami languages by giving a suggestion of their richness yet not introduce too many linguistic barriers for the reader, so that the power, humor, and strangeness of the tales can be absorbed and appreciated.

My warm thanks go to art historian Hanne Abildgaard in Copenhagen; Cuno Bernhardsson at the University Library in Umeå, Sweden; Jonas

Engman at the Nordic Museum Archives in Stockholm; Marlene Hugoson at the Institute for Language and Folklore in Uppsala, Sweden; Ewa Ljungdahl at the South Sami Cultural Center, Gaaltije, in Östersund, Sweden; Vanja Torkelsson, a descendant of Elisabet Rensberg; and to Hugh Beach, Henrik Gutzon Larsen, and Eva Silvén for their support of my projects over the years. I thank Harald Gaski at the University of Tromsø for commenting on my Afterword as well as Coppélie Cocq at the University of Umeå for her detailed notes as a reviewer. I am grateful to the American-Scandinavian Foundation for a travel fellowship that allowed me to conduct research in Uppsala at the Institute for Language and Folklore and in Stockholm at the Nordic Museum Archives, and to the Danish Arts Foundation for their support of the book's publication.

Many thanks to my thoughtful and encouraging editor, Kristian Tvedten, and to Anne Taylor for her meticulous copyediting, as well as to all the dedicated and knowledgeable staff at the University of Minnesota Press.

Introduction

The present small collection of Sami folklore is part of a larger body of material that my husband, Dr. Gudmund Hatt, and I collected together among the Sami in Sweden—as far south as Idre in Dalarna and as far north as the lands of the Karesuando Sami, along with most of the Lapmarks in between. This small collection is being published on its own in the hope it can reach and interest a somewhat larger circle of readers. We expect to publish our broader collection of folklore material in the future, information that in its entirety is likely to be encumbered by many details, different variations of the same story, notes, and so forth, which may be less appealing for the reader who only seeks to get a picture of the Sami way of thinking and who enjoys the charm that comes from folktales and the beliefs of olden times.

I've tried to illustrate a few things in the book, but perhaps some of the pictures, apart from their other shortcomings, also may seem outlandish and almost incomprehensible to those who aren't familiar with life in the tent communities, with the appearance of tents from the inside, and with the clothes worn by the Sami. I try to remedy this by adding to the pictures and text some explanatory notes at the end of the book.

I recorded some of the stories when I lived among the most northerly Swedish Sami in 1907–8, but my husband and I gathered by far the greatest part of them in later trips.

This small book is called "by the fire" because everything here was told around the campfire. Fire is, after the reindeer, the best thing the Sami have. In the old days, fire was a power they made offerings to; they tried not to let it go out. They felt such a personal connection to the trees whose wood they burned, mostly birch and pine, that they chopped "eyes" in the firewood, so the pieces of wood "could see they were burning well." There are still firm rules for how one should lay the firewood on the hearth stones, and if the rules about attending to the fire aren't kept, people, at least the elders, believe that misfortune will follow. For the Sami, the fire is more than light and warmth: it is a "friend and comrade." To be near it means to be secure. Home is where the fire burns.

During the day the Sami, like other people, are busy with tasks. But when the darkness draws them to the campfire, when the stew kettle hangs on its sooty chain and steam and smoke rise through the tent opening to the clouds and night sky, then rest comes, memories slip in, like dreams to a sleeper. The tales and customs of olden times are still a wellspring among the Sami, from which they draw comfort and encouragement to deal with their daily toil. Naturally, here too in Sápmi the springs are almost silted up—modern unculture tosses stones in them and grass grows over them. But if we are fortunate enough to be able to remove what blocks the spring, we can suddenly experience the joy of hearing it.

The faces of young and old light up with smiles of recognition when the right strings are plucked and the music comes: one tells a story, while another adds an important detail. The words spill out, sometimes fantastic and lurid, yet the finest poetry and the purest magic come through as well. The Sami, both young and old, can still tell stories in faith and confidence when they feel secure and understood. The spirit of Fairy Tale perches at the edge of the hearth. The fire hisses, the flames flare and die back, the firelight is divided into light and dark, red and black. Across the tent walls glide huge shapes of people and dogs, fantastically clad men, dogs as clever as humans. The shadows playing around a low-burning campfire are the only proper illustrations for the stories being told. In the protective light everything may be named, all the horror and sorcery conjured by the darkness. Outside in the deepest night wander the dead, the spirits, the evil thoughts one person sends another. Out there live all the horrid sounds; out there are storms and clouds, the moon, stars, and northern lights. Out there are the wild animals, the night and all that is meant by that. Here inside the tent is the campfire; here is home, the great safe place. Only a flimsy turf wall or a tent-cloth wall of wadmal full of holes keeps the dark and everything else out. It's a narrow ring, a small, circular place around a campfire in the wilderness that creates this home—and yes, the same feelings of snugness and cozy comfort exist here, just as in more permanent dwellings.

All that we have heard and seen around this campfire in the wilderness reflects the glow of the flames, a gleam that may cause the object we collected to appear touched with gold, because it was alive in its own surroundings. But for others who didn't see it there, perhaps the object is as gray and dull as an ordinary stone on a country road. The wet stones we collect on the beach are so lovely, yet when we bring them home they're dry and colorless. This is the difference between hearing a "saga" from the goddess Saga's own lips and reading it in a book. Those of us who aren't so fortunate as to be able to travel and collect things must be content with what is retold here.

I thank the Sami people's friend, our common friend, Dr. Hjalmar Lundbohm, because he has offered us steady support and understanding for many years.

Professor K. B. Wiklund has been kind enough to engage with the Sami words and sentences found in this book, for which I am grateful. The treatment of the Sami language has not been easy or completely satisfying work since the present collection of folktales and stories come from almost all the Swedish Lapmarks, and when the Sami dialects are so many and quite different, it has not been possible to merge them into a single speech form. This book does not have philological aspirations, so the Sami words that appear are reproduced in their simplest possible form, without any special phonetic symbols. In the Sami glossary [not included in the English edition], the spelling is greatly simplified, though consideration is given to certain dialects. Those who are interested in linguistics will readily note these, because the locality is always stated in the notes.

In a few instances, the Sami words cannot be identified or translated—for example, i *norrose i gorrose* and *Stallo's gabsteb*. For folkloric reasons, I decided not to omit these words but rather to allow them to stay as we heard them. There are certain rules that talented and sympathetic story-tellers obey—and the Sami are born storytellers. They know these rules without perhaps being aware of them. Children always prefer to hear the same words or the same phrases in particular places in their favorite stories, and so it is in the Sami folktales and legends. Particular phrases and words may be handed down and repeated, while other parts of the narratives are freely altered. Even if a legend is told in Swedish (the southern Sami speak Swedish), some things definitely must be expressed in the Sami language, not because the storyteller momentarily forgets the Swedish words but because these are fixed points in the legend that must not be said in any other way. My translation [into Danish from Swedish and the Sami languages] should follow this style. In this translation I have most often used—even if it's not always the absolute correct choice—the word that has the correct ring for corresponding to the original expression, something the Sami have a fine ear for.

Whatever i *norrose i gorrose* meant to the talented storyteller, it is included here. *Stallo's gabsteb* is allowed to remain as we heard it. The Sami explain that Stallo's language is always strange. "That's how Stallo speaks," they answer when one tries to more closely question the language being used. These simple words and sentences in legend and fairy tale, which are even unclear to the Sami people, most likely are the result of the story traveling from one Sami person to another, through many dialects, but the previously mentioned "fixed points" are supposed to be repeated as nearly as possible in the way they were told originally. When that happens, the sound of the word easily becomes more difficult to understand—and even unintelligible.

The intention of this small book is only to retell some of the legends and stories that are still alive among the Sami. A folkloristic treatment of the material, an attempt to elucidate the different elements, including those that are original to the Sami and those that are generally known and widespread migratory myths, will not be undertaken here.

October 1922

Moose, Lucky Reindeer, Reindeer Luck, and Wizardry

🐌🐌🐌🐌🐌🐌🐌🐌🐌🐌🐌

The Sun's Daughter with the Tame Moose Herd

There was once a young Sami man who had gotten hold of Bejjen neide, the daughter of the sun, in the forest. He saw her watching over her tame moose herd. The lad snuck after her, without her noticing, and took her captive. She followed him peaceably to his tent, along with her tame moose.

She told him how he could hold onto her and her animals. For three nights, he needed to keep the smoke hole covered and also the back entrance to the tent's *boassjo*, or kitchen area; after that, everything would be his. The lad kept the tent covered the first two nights, but on the third night he couldn't stand having the smoke hole covered and so he took off the cloth in the belief that it wouldn't matter very much. But as soon as the sky and stars came into view through the smoke hole, the daughter of the sun said, "Now I see my mother's and father's eyes!" And she disappeared into the air up through the smoke hole. The lad stretched his arms up after her, but she was gone, and her moose with her.

If he had been able to keep her, then neither he nor his relatives would come to suffer want.

And she was so pretty and the sunshine was so beautiful when he saw her walking in the forest with her lovely long hair.

Marja Maria Nilsson, Jämtland

The Sami Who Weren't Satisfied with the Moose

The moose was the first animal the Sami folk had gotten, but it always hung around the tent, where it tramped around, disturbing them. They were also afraid it would knock down the tent because it was so heavy. Then an old Sami woman asked if they couldn't have an easier animal, which would run away from the tent, so the young people would have something to do. This was how the Sami got the reindeer.

Jonas Persson, Härjedalen

The Giant Folk Who Had Tame Moose

Once there were giants living in the mountains who had tame moose, just like the Sami had reindeer. They were the eldest, but another group of people came along that the giants didn't want to live with. The giants arranged their own deaths: they dug deep pits and dressed themselves in their finest and threw themselves into the pits. The moose, the poor moose, grew wild and were persecuted.

Now there are laws so the moose are no longer plagued as cruelly as before. But the reindeer thrive, for they have herders.

Lisbet Nilsdotter, Jämtland

How the Sami Were Given Reindeer and Tents by the Underground Folk and How the Settlers Were Given Farms and Farm Animals

A Sami man was out wandering once in the old days, before the Sami folk had reindeer yet. During this time they lived mostly by snaring ptarmigan. He grew tired and sat down to rest and to eat. As he sat there in the wilderness, a pretty girl came along and sat next to him. He wanted to keep her there, and so he pricked her left little finger with his knife, so it bled. When she saw that, she said, "Oh, that was my heart!" At the same moment an old woman came toward them, and she said to the girl, "Now you have to remain on earth!" The man threw his knife at the old woman to bind her as well, but it didn't reach her, and she disappeared.

The Sami man and the girl lived in a hole in the earth. The girl then said to him that he should remain calm for three days, whatever he saw and heard. Then she vanished from the hole into the mountain wall. It turned eerie around him; he saw queer things and heard strange noises, but he stayed quite calm as the girl had told him to. The second day was worse, and the third day was the worst yet, but the man steadily remained quite calm.

After three days had passed, the girl returned and brought him back up to earth—and up there was a reindeer herd, and there stood a tent with everything necessary.

In this way the Sami folk were given both the reindeer and the tent by the underground folk. Besides that, they also received the lasso and skis.

The man and his wife now began to milk the reindeer. He was supposed to lasso the *aldo*s, or reindeer cows, and hold them steady while she milked. The woman now instructed him that when he worked with the reindeer he must not swear or joke, *i norrose i gorose!*

Yet when the man had lassoed his first *aldo* and it fought against him and bounded away, he could not help himself from uttering an oath, and right away the reindeer fell to the ground, dead. "Oh, misfortune!" cried the woman. When he had caught a second *aldo,* he made sure not to swear when the reindeer resisted him, but he could not stop himself from taking God's name in vain: "Jupmel!" Right away this *aldo* too fell dead to the ground. "Oh misfortune!" cried the woman.

Because of the first reindeer that fell dead when the man swore, the wolf was given the power to tear apart the reindeer, and for the second *aldo* that fell dead when the man took God's name in vain, sickness came among the reindeer.

When the man lassoed the third *aldo* he was silent. Since then, the Sami neither swear nor joke when they work with their herds.

The Swedes have also received their lands and possessions from the underground folk.

They've received farms and fields, cows and sheep and goats, along with fishing tools. This is how it happened:

In the old days, before the Swedes had farms and fields, a Swede was out wandering. By chance he noticed a hole in the earth and thought he could try to go down there.

Below earth was a large farm with fields and meadows. He went into the farmhouse. There stood a table laden with all kinds of food, but he didn't touch any of it. There were also beds, all made up, and in one of them he lay down. A young and then an old woman came to him. He threw his knife over the young girl. "Oh, oh, oh!" she shrieked. She now had to stay with him. He also threw his knife after the old woman, but it missed, and she disappeared.

The young girl bade him remain in the bed for three days and keep calm, no matter what he heard and saw. Noises started up all around him; but he remained calm, even though they became worse and worse. The third day was the very worst of all, but he didn't move. At last the noises slackened, and the girl came back to him and said that he could get up and eat and that the farm and everything were now his.

Margreta Bengtsson, Pite Sápmi

The Old Woman Who Made Reindeer Herding Difficult

In the old days, right after the Sami folk had received the reindeer as their animals, the herd rested quietly at night by the side of the tent, like cows. But there was an old woman who gave her herder a hooded cape to wear and a lasso to drape around his neck. She chased him away, along with the reindeer. Since that time the Sami must guard the reindeer herd in the night as well. And from that time, the Sami have been angry at that old woman, and they have grumbled that she is the reason their lives are difficult, because they always have to guard the reindeer at night.

Anni Rasti, Karesuando

The Sami Lad Who Married a Halde Girl and Was Given Lucky Reindeer Along with Her

A *siida* of Sami reindeer herders had migrated with their reindeer to a new campsite, but not all the herd had followed. A young Sami lad was therefore sent back to retrieve them. He had no difficulty finding them— they were wandering around the campsite and turf hut the *siida* had just left. But the lad grew tired, and he went into the turf hut and lay down to sleep inside the muslin tent he'd brought with him to ward off mosquitos.

As he lay there, two Halde girls arrived, and they teased and tormented him by scratching at his sleeping tent so that he couldn't get any rest. They took turns teasing him; when one stopped, she said to the other, "Now it's your turn, Elle." The Sami lad didn't know what to do to get some peace, but finally he decided to take a sharp needle for sewing leather out of his needle case. With that he stabbed Elle in the hand, so the blood ran. Then the girl broke into tears and said, "Now I can't return to the Halde folk because I've seen my own blood!"

The other girl said, "I'm leaving," and Elle was left on her own. She stood outside the hut and cried. So the Sami lad came out and said that if she could behave properly, she should come inside the hut and be his wife. So she came in, and they built the fire up and lay down to sleep.

In the morning when they were getting ready to leave, the girl's brother arrived with a reindeer herd. The Halde girl's reindeer were to be separated out to form the girl's dowry, now that she was married. Elle said to her husband that he should keep his eye out for a certain large,

She stood outside the turf hut and cried.

handsome reindeer ox during the separation and not let the animal escape from him, however much her brother tried to hinder him, because it was a lucky reindeer.

The Sami lad did look out for and take the large, handsome reindeer ox, but the girl's brother grew very angry about it, for the animal was his best lucky reindeer. When they were finished with the reindeer separation and the girl had her dowry, her brother forbade her ever to return to the campsite where the Sami lad had encountered the girls.

The Sami lad and his Halde wife then moved up to the high mountains with their reindeer, and they became very rich.

Anni Rasti, Karesuando

The Sami lad and his Halde wife then moved up to the high mountains with their reindeer.

How the Sami Girl Tricked the Evil One

A man had promised the Devil, Bærgalak, his daughter in order to get reindeer luck. But the daughter, who knew of her father's promise, protected herself against the Evil One by always keeping "the books" (the Psalms and New Testament) with her, and when she slept she had the Bible under her head. Every time the Devil came to claim his bargain, he said, "Your father has given you to me," but the girl always answered, "I have no other father than God in Heaven." And Bærgalak had to go away empty-handed.

Karesuando

13

The Sami Man and the Devil

Once, in the old days, a man promised himself to Bærgalak, but after the agreed-upon years had passed and the Evil One came to fetch him, the man had worked out a cunning trick to escape. Instead of the usual leather belt that every Sami man wore, he'd sewn for himself a belt from the reindeer's belly fur, with all the hair left on. When Bærgalak asked him to come along, he said, "Yes, if you can count the hairs on my belt." Bærgalak agreed—he thought it was an easy task—but when he saw the furry belt with countless hairs, he understood he was outsmarted and went off, angry and unsatisfied.

Karesuando

Stainak *and the Sami Man Who Died*

There was a man who had a reindeer herd—I don't know how large it was, but it must have been quite large. He actually had a *stainak* in the herd, that is, a rare cow with no calves, which often has bigger than usual antlers. One evening, when they had prevented the calves from nursing, so the *aldos* could be milked later, and the herd was supposed to go out to graze in the night, the man said to his herder that tonight he himself wanted to stand watch so that his servant could lie down to sleep by the corral. There is usually a slope by the corral, and that was where the man wanted the herder to lie down. But the servant suspected that something was wrong and answered, "No, you can sleep there yourself," and said he himself would keep watch on the reindeer that night. The man became quite downcast and said, "Well, I see you don't want to sleep there!"

The reindeer were now driven out of the corral, and the herder followed them. After he had gone a ways, the herd stopped at an open space and quietly began to graze. But suddenly it seemed that the *stainak* wanted to return to the corral, and it did go some distance away from the herd, but not quite back to the corral. It went here and there, bellowing. The herder thought that as far as he was concerned the *stainak* could go wherever it wanted.

In the morning the herder drove the reindeer back to the corral, where they were to be milked. There on the hillside lay the man, looking as if he slept, but when the herder looked more closely, it appeared that his master was dead.

In order to explain the story, I must say that the man had made a pact with an invisible spirit—a good or bad one, I don't know—so that he could have reindeer luck. Now it was likely the agreed-upon period had run out, and the master wanted the herder to go in his place by sleeping where the spirit would be coming to claim his victim, but the servant suspected the truth of the matter and escaped.

The reason the *stainak* carried on so strangely and moved toward the

There on the hillside lay the man, looking as if he slept.

corral in the night was that in certain circumstances the *stainak* has been able to offer its life for that of its owner.

Anders Larsson, Frostviken

The Sami Man Who Wanted His Dead Wife Back

There was a Sami man who was very much in love with his wife, but she died. Her corpse was wrapped up in a sled and placed on a *site*, a high platform supported on poles. The man hadn't completely tied her into the sled; her arms and legs were free. That's because the man was a great shaman, or *noaidi*, and he wanted to try to bring his wife back to life again.

The man was rich: he had a large herd of reindeer and two herders.

He now said to the two herders that they should keep an eye on the corpse and when they saw her raise her hand they should unloose the bonds, so she was completely free. The man went into the tent and lay down to sleep, after placing the big meat fork next to him. So a little time passed, and the two herders out by the high platform saw the corpse raise one hand in the air, but neither of the herders untied her or woke the husband, as he had asked them to do. Either they didn't want to or didn't dare to. After a little more time had passed, the corpse lifted herself halfway up, but since she was bound fast and hadn't been untied yet, she had to remain where she was. The two young herders were actually smarter than they appeared. They suspected that if they untied her, one of them would have to go in her stead.

The two herders out by the high platform saw the corpse raise one hand in the air.

Right afterward, the man woke in the tent. He had been in the spirit kingdom. Down there, his wife stood, already a bride; she was to be married to a ghost. They were in the midst of preparations for the wedding feast. One of the feast goers looked up and saw the man who had arrived. "What can that be? Could it be a sleepwalking seer?"

"No," said another guest, "it's only a heap of stones."

The Sami man kept moving, very softly, and managed to come close, right up behind the bride. He took hold of her and wanted to carry her away with him. There was a great uproar then, and the wedding guests rose and crowded around them.

If at that moment the wicked herders had untied the woman from the sled the man could have surely taken her with him, but now he couldn't get her free because she was still bound up above on the platform. And only with the help of the big meat fork did the *noaidi* himself barely escape from the dead.

Anders Larsson, Frostviken

The Reindeer-Herding Ghost

Two ghosts were out wandering one night when they encountered a Sami man who lay there sleeping. One of them was curious and wanted to observe the man. The other advised him against doing this: "Don't get too near him; he's a powerful *noaidi!*" But his companion didn't obey, and as he came over to the man, the *noaidi* put a curse on him so the ghost had to serve him as a reindeer herder for a year.

The ghost was an unusually adept reindeer herder, quick as the wind and skillful at turning the whole herd around when it ran too far. A reindeer was never lost. Besides that, the ghost had no stomach, so it had no appetite for food. But of course it didn't have a back either, so it couldn't drag trees home to the tent for the fire. He was invisible to everyone but the *noaidi*.

When the year had passed, the ghost was freed from its service and could go to the graveyard again.

Karesuando

The Shoes Sewn from Human Skin

There was a man who gave his servant a pair of shoes on the condition that he should serve the man as long as the shoes lasted but that he must not go to church wearing them.

They were remarkable shoes, and they appeared never to wear out; they lasted many years. The servant finally decided to wear them to church to see what would happen. And as soon as he set foot in the churchyard, the shoes crumbled into pieces. They were made of human skin.

Jon Larsson, Härjedalen

The Wizardly Sami Girl

Two Sami families lived together in the *siida*. In one of the tents were two sons and a daughter versed in the wizardly arts. In the other family were two daughters. The mother of the wizardly daughter would have liked her sons to marry the girls from the other tent, but her daughter didn't like the idea.

Then one day the old *ised*, the foreman of the *siida* and the boys' father, came home from the herd with a reindeer to slaughter. After the reindeer was killed, he went off to sell the meat, and his wife started to make sausage from the reindeer blood. While the *ised* was out selling the meat, the two girls from the neighbor tent came on a visit. The woman offered them some coffee the daughter had made for her father's homecoming, even though the daughter had said to her mother, "Don't give them my coffee; don't expect them to become your daughters-in-law."

Later the *ised* came home after having sold the meat. He lay down to sleep, and his wife and daughter left the tent. When his wife returned she saw, to her great anger, that a pair of goats were inside and they had eaten all the blood sausages. She scolded her husband because he had not paid attention and stopped this, but her daughter said, "You must understand, these are no ordinary goats!" At that time, the Sami people did not like goats. "But here you can see what your daughters-in-law would be like!" With this she let her mother know that she had turned the two Sami girls into goats to show their true nature. That is to say, the goat is the image of a poor and stubborn person.

Anni Rasti, Karesuando

Sickness Spirits

The Sickness Spirit That Arrived on a Stick of Wood

A poor man was on his way to a prosperous Sami tent to ask for a reindeer to slaughter. In those days, when you were poor and had nothing to eat, you sought help only from your own. You never asked for anything from the farmers.

The rich Sami wife was sick, and while the poor man was walking he met on the way a woman he suspected of being a sickness spirit. He entered into conversation with her and asked, if she was going to the same tent where the wife was sick, whether they could walk together. The woman now asked what errand he had in the tent. He said that since he hoped to get an old pack reindeer that he could slaughter, maybe she might get a reindeer cow? She answered that maybe she would rather have an old woman instead.

He asked her more about it, how she was planning to enter the tent. She told him that when the fire chirped the first time, she would be in the vicinity of the tent, and when it chirped the second time she would be near the spot where wood was chopped, and when the fire chirped the third time, she would enter the tent. She would arrive on the tip of a piece of wood that poked out from under the door of the tent, and when she was inside she would place herself between the housewife and the *loaido*, the space around the hearth in the center of the tent, where everyone gathered.

He took the ax and swung it repeatedly into the twig-covered floor in front of the sick woman.

After this conversation they separated, and the man arrived first at the tent. When he had been sitting there a little while, he heard the fire chirp the first time and, soon after, the second time. The poor man now understood that the woman was just outside, near the spot where the wood was chopped. He asked the people in the tent if they had a steel ax. Yes, they did. He asked to borrow it and placed it in front of him.

The family had a daughter in the tent who was a little stiff in the back and for that reason not very careful when placing the wood inside the tent. As usual she had tossed the pieces inside so they fell any old way, such that the ends poked out under the tent door. When more wood was required for the fire and the log was dragged over to the cooking area, the fire chirped the third time. Now the poor Sami knew that the woman had entered and that she was sitting in the *loaido* between the fire and the sick woman. He took the ax and swung it repeatedly into the twig-covered floor in front of the sick woman. Neither he nor the others saw anything, but they clearly heard a moan.

Only afterward did the poor man tell them that he had met a sickness spirit on the way, and he said what she had told him.

This tale has come down from generation to generation, and parents have told it to their children to teach them to pile the wood correctly so that the tips don't poke outside the tent.

Anders Larsson, Frostviken

The Sickness Spirits That Froze in the High Mountains

West of the region of Susendalen there were, many years ago, a number of Sami folk who lived by snaring ptarmigan. An old man was out one day checking his snares when he heard a human voice in the mountains. At first he didn't pay attention to what he heard, but at last it sounded like a sorrowful song. He called out to ask what it was, and it answered. The voices came closer and closer, and when he called out the third time, they came quite near.

There were three. One was fever, the second was smallpox, and the third, plague. The first of the three carried a scythe; the second, a rake; and the third, which was the worst, had a broom.

I don't recall if the old man could see the three people or if he saw only their heads. They now asked him to carry them down to the forest paths; they were freezing up here in the high mountains. The old man at first would not—if they were thinking of killing him, they could just as well do it right away—but they promised they wouldn't do him any harm if only he would carry them down to the hamlet and then return here. They would rather never again come up here to the high mountains.

There were three. One was fever, the second was smallpox, and the third, plague.

The old man carried them down to a farm. When he had come in, he called out to them, and they answered from under the table.

It is said that in the area from Susendalen over to Mosjøen, the people were completely wiped out. Yes, the sickness spirits are just devils that wander under the sun.

Anders Larsson, Frostviken

The Sami Woman Who Saw Fever and Another Sickness Spirit

Anna Sara from Härjedalen tells this story:

Once when I was going home, I met in the woods a tall black-clad woman whom I knew well. When we came close to each other, she turned off and walked into the trees—I heard the twigs break under her footsteps.

When I saw she was bent over and didn't come to me, I called to her several times, but she didn't answer. Now I understood. She resembled the woman I knew who was sick, and I was meeting her sickness. Quite right—she was dead when I came home.

Another time—it was in winter—I was out driving with my reindeer along with a companion. As we came to a crossroads, I saw a Sami man I knew well, standing there. He had tied his reindeer to a birch tree, and over his sled lay a light-colored reindeer pelt. The man was wearing a light-colored reindeer fur tunic. When we drove by, he turned his back to us. I thought that he also intended to go to the *siida*, and when I returned home I said he was on his way to us. But my father said, "No, that can't be. You know that for some while he has had a bad leg and can't even walk." Of course that was true. I had completely forgotten that, but it still must have been him, because I saw him so plainly. Then I described exactly what he was wearing and everything, to the great amazement of my travel companion—he hadn't seen anything at all. But my father said, "You saw 'the fever,' and luckily it wore a light color, so it won't turn deadly."

A short time after that the Sami man I thought I'd seen became ill and after that several others, and finally everyone became ill. No one died, but they were very ill and delirious, so that it was always necessary to make sure they didn't get too close to the fire in the tent.

Anna Sara, Härjedalen

Murdered Children

The Dead Child Who Came to Life Again

There was a young Sami man and his sweetheart who had a baby together. She gave birth in the wilderness, and he killed the baby after the mother had first half-strangled it. He then took her scissors and put them, open, in the baby's mouth so it wouldn't cry. In those days no one knew what to do to silence the ghost of a murdered baby, an *epper*. Then they placed the dead baby, with the scissors in its mouth, in the crevice of a rock.

Afterward, the young couple married. One day the wife missed her scissors; she needed to use them and none were to be found in the tent.

"Why don't you go and take the scissors we left with the child in the crevice?" said the husband.

So the wife went to look for the scissors. At first she couldn't find the place. Finally she did find it, but when she took the scissors, the dead child suddenly rose up, grabbed the scissors, and stabbed the mother in the neck, killing her.

Afterward the *epper* went to the tent of its father's sister and said, "Good day, my aunt."

"Good day, good day, my boy," she answered. The aunt was in the midst of bathing her own child. "Come, my boy, I'll wash you in your cousin's bathwater," she said.

But when she took the scissors, the dead child suddenly rose up.

"I am going first to greet my father," said the baby.

"I hope you're not going to harm your father and mother?" she said, not knowing yet that he had already killed his mother.

"No, I won't, if he greets me," said the *epper*.

The *epper* went to his father's tent and stood inside the door and said, "Good day, my father!" But the father was so shocked that he didn't answer, and in his terror he got under the sheepskin coverlet and hid his head among the bedclothes. Now the *epper* jumped on his father and broke his back. After that the father was an invalid for life.

The *epper* returned to his aunt's tent and stood inside the door. He breathed hard and moaned as he said, "I have just finished dealing with my father and my mother."

Now the aunt asked, "I hope you haven't harmed your father and mother?"

Then the *epper* told her how his parents had murdered him and how he now in revenge had killed his mother and broken his father's back.

So the aunt said again, "Come, my boy, I'll wash you in your cousin's bathwater!" And now he came over and was washed in the bathwater. With that he became a real, living child, and she christened him and

So the aunt said again, "Come, my boy, I'll wash you in your cousin's bathwater!"

called him Epper. After that time all abandoned babies were called Epper.

He grew up with his aunt and lived like a real human. He was just a little different from other Sami in that he had a rather large head. It came from his aunt not having formed his head when she bathed him—precisely so that it should be a sign he was an *epper*.

Epperpardne, Epper-boy, he was called as a child, and later they called him *Epper-poatnjekutj, Epper-man* (which means that he also married, for *poatnjekutj* means husband).

This was the Epper who taught his aunt the practice that all Sami women have observed since then: to use the same bathwater for three days and then pour it off under the father's hearthstone in the tent, so that the children left out to die and now buried under the earth can wash themselves in it.

Since those days it has become known that baptizing exposed children gives them peace. You call out a name and the christening formula in the direction that the child's scream can be heard.

But no one knows if any other woman has been brave enough to take in an *epper* and bathe it.

Margreta Bengtsson, Pite Sápmi

Epper

A *siida* migrated once between Dorothea and Vilhelmina over Blaikfjeldet, a flat, even-topped mountain that is a good six miles long. The reindeer herd went first, and after the herd followed the caravans with people and their goods. Among the migrating Sami was an old man, who sat in his sled. A storm was in the air and a plaintive voice could be heard, which came closer and closer to the caravans. Now, there was in the *siida* a young married couple, and the old man, who heard the dead baby scream, called out loudly to the caravans: "Who is the baby's mother?"

No one answered. Then the invisible death spirit broke the mother's back, and the young woman was from that moment paralyzed. If she had answered and acknowledged she was the mother of the baby, nothing bad would have happened to her.

Anders Larsson, Frostviken

Animals

How the Sami Got the Dog

The Sami first had the white fox for a dog, but it wasn't of much use; it only ran around killing the reindeer calves. After that they tried to turn the red fox into their helper, but it only ran after the reindeer without barking, and it also killed the calves. The third animal the Sami tried to make a helper was the wolverine. It was better than the other two; it barked and also directed the herd, but all the same it killed one or two reindeer.

One day, when the husband was not home, just the wife, the wolverine came to the tent and stole food. It broke open a *gisa* and ate everything in it. The wife became angry and thrashed the wolverine. The wolverine now grew angry and ran off. A while later the husband returned to the tent and asked after the "dog," and the wife told him that she had chased it away because it stole. The husband went off, calling for it, but the wolverine answered, "From now on, I'm only going to live in the wilderness and tear the reindeer to pieces." The husband later went to see what the wolverine was up to, and he saw it was killing reindeer. So the husband killed the wolverine. From that day the Sami and the wolverine were enemies.

Then one day when the woman was out herding, she saw her dog running. It began to help her by barking: *Viv, viv, viv!* She now saw that the dog was an excellent helper, and she wanted to lure the dog by

And she wanted to lure the dog by giving it a piece of meat from her own food stock.

giving it a piece of meat from her own food stock that she kept inside the tent. At first, the dog didn't dare take it, but then she offered the dog a meat bone and the dog took the bone. The woman now began to speak to the dog about going into service with them as a reindeer herder. But she was afraid that the dog would want to be paid too much. "Don't be afraid of that," said the dog. "Just give me some soup and the bones, and then I will be satisfied." After that, the dog served the Sami as a reindeer herder.

Margreta Bengtsson, Pite Sápmi

Dogs with Different Natures

Two dogs, who each served a different mistress, began to speak about their food. "My mistress always gives me the fat in the soup," said one of them, "and bones with meat on them."

"That's something my mistress doesn't do, right enough," said the other dog. "She is so miserly that I have to steal to keep body and soul together."

The dog that was given bad food and that stole barked only a little and was a lazy worker. But the dog given good food barked loudly and did his work well.

From that time there have been two kinds of dogs, some that bark loudly and are skilled at their work and others that steal and are lazy and only bark feebly.

Margreta Bengtsson, Pite Sápmi

The Reindeer and Sheep Race to the Farmer's House

The reindeer and the sheep are brothers. They resemble each other; they are both easily frightened. When a sheep loses its way, it goes to the mountains, against the wind, just as the reindeer does, all the way up into the high mountains.

The sheep and the reindeer decided to race to see which of them would get to the farmer's house first. The reindeer was indeed the faster, so it got there first, but the sheep was craftier, so it called out to the reindeer: "Brother, brother, look at your white tail!" The reindeer turned around to look at its tail, and it ran around in circles trying to get a glimpse. And meanwhile the sheep slipped into the farm.

That was how it happened that the sheep became a domestic animal while the reindeer continued to belong to the wilderness.

Jämtland

The Bear That Carried Jesus over the River

While God was in the midst of creating the animals, a few of them were standing in a bog. Jesus came along and wanted to cross the river. He asked the reindeer to carry him across: "If you do it you'll be able to rest all night without needing to eat." The reindeer merely sneezed and went his way, saying: "I couldn't live through a whole night without needing to eat." Then Jesus said, "You will have to search for your food in the high mountains, and it will be difficult for you digging through the snow in winter to find it. You will lose all your hair, and the wolf, the fox, and all the other animals will hunt you down and tear you to pieces!" (though not the hare or the sheep, for they are the reindeer's relatives).

Jesus then asked the moose to carry him across, but the moose didn't have time either, as it was looking for food. Therefore, it was also to have difficulty with finding food and would need to eat birch leaves. When Jesus asked the sheep to carry him across, it just stood there and gaped: *Njim, njim, njim!* It was busy eating, and because of that the sheep must always eat.

Jesus asked the horse to carry him over the river, but it excused itself by saying it had such round feet that it was afraid of sliding on the smooth stones in the water. So the horse became man's slave and had always to go in harness.

There sat the bear listening to all this, and it said, "Get up on my back. My legs are perhaps a little short to wade in the river, but I have such sharp claws on my feet that I can probably stand fast on the stones." The bear carried Jesus over the river. As payment for that, the bear was given the right to sleep all winter without needing to eat. Only once during mid-winter does the bear wake to turn over on its other side and go on sleeping. But the bear has promised never to kill human beings. If it does kill a human being, its wintertime sleep is over.

Margreta Bengtsson, Pite Sápmi

When God Doled Out Fat to the Animals

God once doled out fat to the animals. He put the fat on a *dælo*, a reindeer skin used as a tablecloth. When he only had a few bits left, the hare came to get his share of the fat. God told the hare that it could roll on the tablecloth, but the hare thought there was too little fat and went his way without getting anything. That's why the hare is so thin. Then the bear came to get some fat. God also told the bear that it could roll itself in the bits of fat. The bear did as God said; that is the reason it is one of the fattest animals.

Kristoffer Klementsson, Västerbotten

The Fastest Animals

When humans were created, they were faster than all others; they could capture the reindeer, the wolf, and each and every one of the wild animals that God had created. But then the red fox said, "This will not do, that people are so fast, for now they will kill all the animals." Our Lord took the fox's advice, and people then became the slowest of them all.

The red fox thought that now it was the fastest of all the animals, and it boasted, "I am the fastest!" But the white fox said, "No, I am the fastest!" They decided to compete in running after the fleeing reindeer. The white fox won; it even managed to run twice around the wild reindeer before the red fox had captured it. On this occasion the red fox had to give up.

Jouna Rasti, Karesuando

The Woodpecker

The woodpecker has been sentenced to search for its food in the trees. There was once a farm woman who was baking bread when God came and asked her for bread. She gave him a tiny little piece, but from that God made a large, large cake. When the farm woman saw it, she swore at him and called him a wizard. But then God sentenced her to have to search for food in the trees. The farm woman thus became a woodpecker, and since she was wearing a checked dress, the woodpecker became speckled.

Härjedalen

The Loon

The loon was angry with God because he didn't give him red feet. The loon flew away, offended, but as it flew, God threw its legs after it. Thus the legs came to sit too far back, so the bird cannot walk. That is the reason it builds its nest so near the water, so it can just jump in.

The loon was given its ugly, unpleasant voice as punishment for killing a human. It was a man who had set a snare for the loon and caught it. But when he wanted to take it out, the bird attacked him and stabbed his sharp beak into the man's heart. Since then, the loon has had the man's death shriek.

Margreta Bengtsson, Pite Sápmi

The Hazel Grouse

In the old days, when the animals were created, the hazel grouse was the largest of all the animals. But then one day, when God came to take a look at the animals, it happened that the grouse suddenly flew up so it surprised God, and he gave a start. Then God thought, "That bird is too big. I will make it smaller."

God then divided up the grouse among all the other animals. Each of them has therefore a piece of the grouse's flesh. The reindeer has grouse flesh at its throat. The fish have a little bit of grouse flesh in their heads, under the lower jaw. The birds all have some of the grouse's flesh in front of the breastbone.

Kristoffer Klementsson, Västerbotten

How Mosquitos Came into the World

After God had created mosquitos, he stuffed all of them into a sack, and then he left them in the care of a Sami woman. Eventually she grew so tired of hearing the constant buzzing of the mosquitos that in the end she couldn't stop herself from letting a few out, just a very few, so that the buzzing would stop. But all the mosquitos flew out at her and flew everywhere and stung man and beast. She ran every which way to capture them in the sack again, but it was all in vain. The mosquitos spread around the world.

Probably when God gave her the sack to take care of, he thought she would get sick of their buzzing and, sooner or later, let them out.

Jämtland

Origins of Lice

There was an old Sami woman who asked the earth to get some lice, so that she could have something to do on Sundays, and so that people's clothing shouldn't remain too dirty, because when the clothes have too many lice, of course they must be washed. And Sundays are just the time to delouse.

Margreta Bengtsson, Pite Sápmi

The Pike Fish and the Snake

The snake and the pike both lived in the water, but then they made a pact that whichever of them could first swim to an agreed-upon headland should be allowed to live in the water forever, while the one who came last should live on land.

They swam, and the pike won the race. "It is a good thing indeed that I came first," said the pike, "because if I had ended up living on land, I would have killed people."

The pike is in fact a far more dangerous animal than the snake.

Margreta Bengtsson, Pite Sápmi

Dangerous to Sleep by a Juniper Bush

You must not lie down to sleep outside close to a juniper bush, for if a lizard is accidentally frightened, it will look for the nearest hole it finds, and you can easily risk it running into your mouth and down into the stomach, and there it can multiply. That's what happened to a farm woman I know, but she followed this advice and recovered:

Bake rye bread, and while it is still warm and fragrant, place the loaf on the table. After that, support your chin on the edge of the table and hold your mouth open over the loaf. The smell of the fresh bread tempts the lizard out. First comes the mother, and afterward she fetches one baby after the next. The farm woman needed to be patient until they all had come up. With this advice, the woman grew quite well.

Jämtland

The Woman Who Wanted to Help the Frog

A Sami woman saw an adder and a frog fighting with each other. She wanted to help the frog and gave a blow to the adder but missed and hit the frog. So the frog jumped up on her foot, which immediately swelled and thickened. But the adder came over to her, and it wound itself three times around the bad foot, which immediately was well and no longer swollen.

It was summer when this happened, when she had walked a short ways from the tent.

Anna Sara, Härjedalen

Snake Cure

There was a Sami man whose wife became so sick that he had to give up migrating with the reindeer and to buy a little settler cabin instead.

The wife grew weaker and weaker and so heavy that she filled up the entire bed. One spring day, when the children played outside the house, they saw a snake appear; it was about two feet in length and thin as a finger, but with a thicker head. It crept up a birch. "See how it's crawling to you!" said their father.

He thought it must mean something that the snake appeared. Now the children wanted to fell the tree so they could catch the snake, but it crept down on its own and settled itself in a ring around the foot of the tree. The father then hit the snake on its head, so it was half dead; after that he held down the snake's head with a cleft branch so it opened its mouth wide and stuck its tongue out. He cut off the poison stinger (the tongue). When that was done he brought the snake inside and placed it on his wife's naked body. The snake began to wind itself around her and to suck on her until she fainted. At the same time the woman grew thinner and thinner and the snake grew thicker and thicker and bright red. After a short while the snake died. The man took the snake carefully away to a little lake and threw its tongue after it. Immediately the snake came back to life and took its tongue. When the man and the children returned to the house, the woman was completely restored to health. The children joiked for joy that their father had healed their mother. Some of the children are still alive.

Margreta Bengtsson, Pite Sápmi

The Great Mother Frog

Once there were children who were playing with a frog; they slaughtered it and cut it into pieces and hung the pieces up, the way one does with reindeer meat. Suddenly an amazingly large frog appeared from under the stones. It had big, bulging eyes and stared intensely at the children. They were so frightened that they ran home and told everyone. Among the adults was Johan Biettar, whom I knew. Now he is dead. His father, a *noaidi*, was there, and when he heard what the children had to say, he went to the great frog and conjured it away, perhaps by speaking kindly to it and asking it for forgiveness and explaining that they were only children who had done it. This was the Great Mother Frog, who had appeared in order to take revenge.

Anni Rasti, Karesuando

The Fox Tricks the Bear and Makes a Sami Man Rich

The fox had stolen some fish from a man. And just as he was walking along with his catch, he met the bear, who saw the delicious fish and asked where one could find such a catch. The fox answered that the bear should stick his tail in the waterhole that people drew water from. Here the fish would cling to his tail and he would need only to pull them up, but they bit best in a strong frost. The bear stuck his tail in such a waterhole and waited patiently until the tail was frozen fast. He believed it was the fish hanging on to it. Suddenly the fox cried, "People are coming! People are coming!" The bear sprang up to flee and jerked the frozen tail so hard that it tore off.

Now the bear was angry at the fox and caught it and carried it off in its jaws to kill it. In this difficult situation, the fox began to talk to the bear as if nothing had happened. But the bear could not answer because he had the fox between its teeth. Finally, when the fox asked eagerly,

42

"What wind have we today?" the bear said, "The North Wind!" With these words he had to relax his grip, and the fox was free.

The fox did not get far though before the bear caught him again. And once again the fox began to talk, as if to himself. "Oh the times were better then, when I decorated the skins of small birds," said the fox as they passed a colorful woodpecker in a tree.

"Couldn't you make my skin as beautifully colored as that?" growled the bear.

"Yes, I surely could, but it will hurt. You wouldn't be able to stand the pain."

"Yes I can. I can easily stand it," said the bear.

"Oh, but there's so much work involved. You have to dig a big pit and trees have to be pulled up and a fire lit in the pit and willow branches must be twined together."

"I can do all that," said the bear, and he started work right away. The bear huffed and puffed, managing to dig the pit, gather the wood and set it alight, place logs over the pit, and twine the willow branches. Then the fox got ready to decorate the bear's skin. The fox carefully bound the bear fast to the logs with the twined willows. The bear, who began to find it warm when the fire singed his fur, cried, "Hot, hot, old fox!"

"Yes, I knew you couldn't stand having your back decorated."

"I can stand it, I can stand it!" cried the bear.

But the bear burned up, so only the legs were left. The fox collected them in a sack and he walked off, rattling them as he walked. A Sami man who came by bought the sack in exchange for six of his pack reindeer. The fox had made him believe that there was a treasure in the sack but that he must not open the sack to look inside before he passed seven small hills, or else the treasure would be transformed into burned legs. The man went off with the sack and the fox with the reindeer.

The fox wanted the reindeer slaughtered, and so he called together the other animals to help him. When all the reindeer were killed, the

"Hot, hot, old fox!" cried the bear, when the fire singed his fur.

fox scared all his helpers away by shouting that people were coming. The animals fled in all directions, but the wolf snatched a reindeer leg to take with him. The wolf always attacks the reindeer by sinking its teeth in the reindeer's haunch. The wolverine took the head; it always goes for the reindeer's head. But the hare ran in fear under the sooty stewpot, and with that, the tips of his ears turned solid black. The fox was now alone with the reindeer meat and was just about to eat when the Sami man, whom he had deceived, came back to kill the fox. The fox suggested that instead of killing him, the man and the fox should go to the king's estate. There the fox would make the man rich.

When they arrived at the king's estate, the fox went in first to the king and said to him, "I have a rich man with me, but he doesn't dare come in because he doesn't have a change of clothes with him." So the king gave the fox some beautiful clothes, and the fox brought them to the Sami and bade him put them on. After that, they returned to the king. The fox now told the king that the man was so rich he had 500 tree cutters and 500 field hands working for him. The fox suggested that the king should give his daughter to this rich man.

The king agreed with this, and the man was wed to the king's daughter. After they were married, the king wished to see his son-in-law's great property. The fox ran off to prepare for this. He knew there was a little snake that owned a large estate and had 500 tree cutters and 500 field hands working for him. The fox went to him. First he met the 500 tree cutters and to them he said, "The king is coming and wants to kill you, but if you say you are his son-in-law's tree cutters, he won't do you any harm." They promised to say that when the king came. After that the fox said the same thing to the 500 field hands, that the king was coming to kill them but if they said that they were his son-in-law's field hands, then they would save their lives. And they fell in with this.

Finally the fox came to the snake's house, and there he met the maidservant: "The king is coming and wants to kill you, but if you say you serve the king's son-in-law, then nothing bad will happen to you."

The maid promised to say that, whereupon the fox asked, "Where is the snake?"

"He is sitting in the dining room at the table," said the maidservant.

The fox went into the dining room and said to the snake, "The king is coming and wants to kill you!"

"Where shall I go then?" said the snake, terrified. The fox answered, "Here is a roll of homespun cloth; I'll put you in it and put you up on the shelf."

"Yes, do that," bade the snake.

So the fox rolled the snake up in the roll of homespun and threw the

Folktales

∩∩∩∩∩∩∩∩∩∩∩

Njavisjædne and Atsisjædne

Njavisjædne was a good person, but Atsisjædne wasn't a good person at all. Njavisjædne had a son and a daughter, but Atsisjædne only had a daughter. They lived in the same *siida,* and one day, when they went out to pick berries, Atsisjædne said, "Whichever of us fills the berry bowl first will get the boy child." Njavisjædne agreed, and they began to pick berries. Atsisjædne made a bundle of twigs and leaves and put it at the bottom of the milking cup that she was using as a berry bowl, and on top she placed the berries. With that, she filled her bowl long before Njavisjædne, who picked in the normal way. So Atsisjædne took the boy, and Njavisjædne got Atsisjædne's daughter instead of her own son.

Atsisjædne and Njavisjædne each lived on their own side of Bassevare, the Holy Mountain. The boy grew up to become an excellent hunter of wild reindeer, so in Atsisjædne's tent there was always an abundance of meat and fat, while in Njavisjædne's tent they had to boil soup from the legs of old boots. Atsisjædne was so extravagant that she used the fatty membrane of the reindeer for an apron and the fat of the intestines as a neckerchief. Besides that, she used pieces of meat as logs placed inside the two entrances to the tent. And when the young man went hunting, she always said to him, "My dear boy, never go to the other side of the Holy Mountain. Terribly bad people live there."

All the same, one day he went to the other side of the Holy Mountain. Before going he had stuck into his tunic a piece of reindeer fat.

47

"My dear boy, never go to the other side of the Holy Mountain. Terribly bad people live there."

When he encountered Njavisjædne's tent, he crept quietly up to the top of it and peeked through the smoke hole. They sat down there boiling soup from the bootlegs. He slipped a little piece of fat into the stewpot without anyone noticing. A bit later, Atsisjædne's daughter said, "Listen, mother, the stewpot is bubbling with fat!" Njavisjædne answered, "So you think the stewpot could be bubbling with fat, after your mother took my son and tossed you aside?" With that, the lad realized that Njavisjædne was his real mother, not Atsisjædne.

He went back to Atsisjædne, and as he came in, he said, "Build up a very large fire. I'm freezing." She did this, but he asked her to make it even bigger. When the fire was really large, he threw Atsisjædne into the

flames. As she burned up, she cried, "My dear boy, don't burn the mother who has nursed you!" After that he went to his own true mother's tent and stayed there. And now the mother and children lived together and were happy.

Eventually Njavisjædne died, and they buried her alongside the tent.

Anni Rasti, Karesuando

The Daughters of Njavisjædne and Atsisjædne

One day, when both girls were on their way to church, there stood a goat on a rock, and it said, "Dear girl, milk me and wash your hands in the milk!"

Atsisjædne's daughter answered, "I don't want to soil my hands for church," and she walked on.

The goat said the same thing to Njavisjædne's daughter, and she milked the goat and washed her hands in the milk. Immediately she received clothes that shone like the sun and that could light up a dark house. When she came into the church, she glowed like the brightest sunshine. In the church was the son of a king, who saw her and wanted her for his wife, but he could never get close enough to her to have a conversation. This went on Sunday after Sunday, and he was never able to get any closer. So he tarred the floor where she was accustomed to sit. And the following Sunday as she was leaving the church, one of her shoes remained stuck in the tar. The king's son took the shoe and followed her so he would know where she went.

Some time later he went to where they lived, but it was a weekday and Njavisjædne's daughter was not wearing her sunshine clothes. As the king's son came inside the house with the shoe, the daughter of Atsisjædne cried, "That is my shoe, bring it here!" The king's son gave her the shoe, but it was too small, and she went outside and chopped off part of her foot with an ax so it could fit into the shoe. Then a little bird sang, "The sweetheart of the king's son walks with a bloody foot!" And immediately the king's son saw who the right one was, even though she wasn't wearing her sunshine clothes. He knew her and wed her and stayed there.

They were married for a year and had a child. Then the king's son wrote home to his father that he had a wife whose clothing shone like the sun; she could light up a dark house. The king wrote to his son and asked him to come for a visit with his wife.

The king's son traveled with the whole family. When they were so near the king's estate that they could see it, Njavisjædne's son called out, "Little sister, listen, put on your finest clothes, the king's estate is in view!"

"What did our brother say?" asked Njavisjædne's daughter.

Atsisjædne's daughter was quick to answer, "He said, 'Put on your best clothes and jump into the sea.'" So her sister put on her sunshine clothes and jumped into the sea.

The king now came driving toward them in a gold coach, but as soon as Atsisjædne's daughter sat inside it, it broke to pieces. When they arrived at the king's estate, the king had arranged for the house to be dark, but his daughter-in-law did not shine at all.

So their brother took the child and went down to the shore and called, "Come, little sister and nurse your child; the child is crying, and the cow's milk is bloody."

His sister came to the shore and nursed the child, but it was very difficult for her to come, and she went straight back to the sea again. Sometime later her brother went to the sea and called his sister forth with the same words. This time it was even more difficult for her to come, but she did come and nursed the child, and before she went back, she told her brother that the sea-man had captured her and he would not let her slip away to the shore yet another time.

Her brother now went to the king's son and told him what had happened, and they didn't know what to do, but they went down to the old Halde who sat by the water. She advised them that the brother should make a suit of clothes that three people could fit into, and then they should go down to the shore and call the sister up as before. When she came up, the brother was to throw the suit of clothing over his sister and the king's son at the same time, so they were all inside it at once. They were not to worry about whatever horrible animals and ghosts they saw. Eventually the *draugen,* or sea-monster, would appear as a large rock on shore, and this they should pick up and throw into the sea.

The brother did all as the Halde had told him, and everything happened as it was supposed to. After that all three journeyed up to the king's estate, and Njavisjædne's daughter illuminated everything with her sunshine clothes.

Then one Sunday Njavisjædne's daughter and Atsisjædne's daughter went to church together. On the way they came to a place where some-one stood with their basket of grain, which Atsisjædne's daughter over-turned. Njavisjædne's daughter began to gather the grain since she could not stand to see it go to waste.

Atsisjædne's daughter went into the church, and the church burned, and she burned up.

Anni Rasti, Karesuando

Atsisjædne Tars the Moon

Atsisjædne was a Sami woman in olden days who was so bad-tempered and malicious that she beat her reindeer with the milking cup when she milked. Thus all her reindeer turned into wild reindeer, and she herself became a beetle, *atsisjædne*. When her reindeer went wild, the reins got tangled and the bundle of reins was to be found up in the birch trees. Since her reindeer were gone, she wanted to steal some tame reindeer from the Sami, but the moon was shining and to conceal her deed, she took a pail of pitch and began to tar the moon black. The pitch sucked her in, and there she is still.

Anni Rasti, Karesuando

The Poor Lad Who Rescued the Princess

In the king's town it used to be that every seventh year the church key went missing. People searched, but no one could find it.

The king had three daughters, but the two eldest had been kidnapped by Stallo, and no one knew where they were. A poor young lad courted the youngest princess, but the king was angry about his courtship. One day he gave the lad a letter to take to his captain, and in the letter he wrote that the captain should kill the lad.

As the lad was walking with this letter, he met an old Halde. She asked to see the king's letter, and when she had read it, she told him how the land lay, and she rewrote the letter so he would not come to harm. When the king saw he was still alive, he promised the lad his daughter if he could tell the king where the church key was and bring him back his two kidnapped daughters.

Now the king thought he would be rid of the boy. The lad went on his way dejectedly, but again he met the old Halde on the path, and she told him where to go to find Stallo. He should go to the sea, and there a Sea-Halde would help him.

In this way the lad discovered Stallo's estate—Stallo himself was out fishing. As the lad entered the house, he saw one of the king's daughters: she was now Stallo's maidservant. The lad explained how things were and bade her closely question Stallo as to what had become of her sister and where the church key was.

However, Stallo had Aaron's rod—a heavy weapon that he could only lift if he drank himself strong with a magic potion he had in a flask. When the lad had gone out, Stallo came home to eat, and he was in haste to leave again. He smelled human blood straight away and started to search, but the maid pricked one of her fingers and showed him the blood; that was what he smelled. Now, while Stallo was eating, she began to question him. Well, yes, he had hidden her sister in a bottle, so that she could remain young and serve him as a maid when the first sister had become too old and worn-out. And the church key lay under a large stone by the side of the church.

When Stallo had gone off fishing again, the lad returned and took the rod and the strengthening medicine, all of Stallo's treasure, and both girls, and he started homeward. When Stallo discovered they were gone, he set after them; but the Sea-Halde swallowed him up, and they managed to get home.

When the king saw all the treasure the lad had gotten, he set off to the Sea-Halde to find riches, but the Sea-Halde swallowed him, and he never returned. The poor lad, who was now rich, married the youngest princess.

When folk tried to find the church key where it was supposed to be, under the stone, the stone was so heavy and large that no one could budge it. They called in the lad, who drank from his strengthening potion and then easily lifted up the enormous stone, and there lay the key to the church right enough. And now there was great joy in the city.

Karesuando

Jerusalem's Shoemaker

When God's son walked the earth and carried all of humanity's heavy sins on his shoulders, he once came to the house of a rich man. He leaned against the wall of the farm to ease his burden a little. Then the rich man came out and chased him away. From that time the evil man was cursed. He had to walk without rest on bare feet until the world ended. He couldn't reach the shoes that he bore on his back, only snatch at them.

Once he came to Sápmi, and there he met a reindeer herder, who came from the east, and he asked the herder, "Does the cuckoo still call in the spring?"

"Yes, it does," answered the herder.

Once he came to Sápmi, and there he met a reindeer herder, who came from the east.

"Does the reindeer still grow new antlers each year?"

"Yes, it does," answered the herder.

"Is the everlasting flower still alive?"

"Yes, it is," said the herder. So the man who was not allowed to rest had to journey on.

He had to ask those questions; for when the cuckoo no longer calls in the spring, and when the reindeer does not get new antlers, and when the everlasting flower fades, then the end of the world is coming, and he will have peace.

Karesuando

The Dog-Turk

My father told the story that, when Tromsø was not yet a true city, a pair of Sami girls lived there. One day a Russian ship came and stole them. The Russians sold them to the Dog-Turk, and he started to fatten them up to eat later. Every day he came and stabbed them with a fingernail to see if they were fat enough. As long as blood came off on his fingers after stabbing them, the girls were not fat enough. One of the girls ate the food the Dog-Turk offered, but the other barely touched it.

One day, when the Dog-Turk was out in his tobacco field, the thin girl killed his house servant. The Dog-Turk saw this from his field, and so he came home, took the fat girl, bound a handkerchief around her eyes, and carried her out to the slaughtering place where he murdered her.

The thin girl escaped into the tobacco field, where she hid herself. The Dog-Turk did not have the heart to crush his tobacco plants by going after her. The girl remained there a whole week; she had taken food with her. After that she escaped up a river, whose water erased her tracks. Higher up, she reached a waterfall. There she hid herself in the empty space under the fall, inside the rock. The Dog-Turk understood she had escaped, but he knew that she couldn't get over the waterfall, and he waited for her to show herself again. But after he had waited a week, he decided she was dead, and he went home again.

Meanwhile the girl had moved farther away, and over on the other bank of the river she met some people at war with each other. She asked them to help her and said whichever side helped her would win the battle. One side promised to help her, and so they won the battle. Then they managed to get her on board a ship that took her back to Tromsø. And the girl was saved from the Dog-Turk.

The storyteller has heard this story from her father, and her grandfather saw the girl. The storyteller believes she has seen a living Dog-

Turk in Tromsø. The Dog-Turk has the muzzle of a dog but otherwise is like a human being. All the same, she added:

"But do you really think the Dog-Turk still exists?"

Anni Rasti, Karesuando

The Dog-Turk Lost His Prey

Another time, Bænadurkki, the Dog-Turk, captured a pair of Sami children, a twelve-year-old girl and a boy, when they were skiing on a mountain slope.

The Dog-Turk brought both children home to his brother and their old mother, who kept house for them. The children were each put in their own pen for fattening up. One day when both the Dog-Turks went out to do some stealing, they told their old mother to start a fire in the oven and roast the girl child for their evening meal when they came home to eat. Then they left, and the old woman lit a fire in the oven. When the wood was reduced to burning coals, she bade the girl rake out the coals, saying she herself was so old and feeble that she could not manage to handle the long oven rake. The little girl, who understood well enough what this meant, jumped up and pushed the old woman into the glowing oven and roasted her and prepared her for dinner for the two Dog-Turks. When this was done, she fetched her brother, and both children hid in the cellar.

When the Dog-Turks came home for their dinner, they soon saw what had happened, and angrily they began to search for the children. They did not think to search the cellar. They ran straight to the tobacco fields and hunted there, without finding them. It had now become dark, and they couldn't search any longer so went home to sleep. The children crept up from the cellar and dashed out into the large tobacco fields, where there is such a strong smell of tobacco that the Dog-Turks have difficulty tracking anyone there. In the morning one of the Dog-Turks came to search again for them, by which time the children had gotten over the river to the other side, where they had found shelter with good people at a farmhouse.

The Dog-Turk had jumped over the river and tracked the children up to the farm, but he did not dare to pursue them any farther. And so the children got away home.

Anni Rasti, Karesuando

Jættanas, Who Wanted a Sweetheart

The giant Jættanas was incredibly strong; we still have the expression "strong as Jættanas." One time Jættanas thought he might like a sweetheart. He saw a Sami man sitting and cuddling his girl up in the forest by the banks of a lake. Jættanas, who was a terribly strong rower, now set off in his boat across the lake with such speed that the boat dashed up on land about a hundred lengths. The man became so frightened that he climbed up a tall pine tree so fast that the pine fell over, and in the fall it knocked over Jættanas, and the man hurriedly cut out the giant's eyes. With that, the Sami man and his sweetheart escaped from Jættanas.

Jouna Rasti, Karesuando

The Boy Who Killed Stallo

There was once a Sami boy who was helping Stallo carry a large bag of money. The boy managed it, however, so that it was Stallo who ended up carrying both him and the bag. At long last they came to a steep cliff, and the boy suggested they sit down and rest a while with their legs out over the edge, as if they were on a bench. Stallo was rather tired and sat down willingly. "Sit a little farther out," said the lad, "then you'll be more comfortable!" Stallo moved to the rim of the abyss in good faith. But

Stallo moved to the rim of the abyss in good faith.

then the boy pushed him with all his strength, and Stallo fell down and was killed.

Afterward the lad went his way with the bag of money.

Southern Västerbotten

Stallo Plays Blind Man's Bluff

One time Stallo played blind man's bluff with the Sami on a frozen lake. Stallo was "it," and the Sami ran and leaped around him. At last they jumped over a hole in the ice, and when Stallo set out after them he fell in the water with a splash. He could not get out, and so he called for his drinking tube to drink the lake dry. But the Sami gathered and watched out for the drinking tube. When it flew through the air, they grabbed it.

Then Stallo called for his ax. But the Sami were ready for that too and took the ax when it flew through the air. Finally Stallo tried to spring up from the bottom of the lake through the hole in the ice, but he did not hit the hole. The ice rose in a great bulge where he collided with it—and Stallo drowned.

Västerbotten

Stallo Loses His Prey

Once when Stallo had captured some Sami children he put them in his boat, lifted the boat onto his shoulder, and journeyed home to eat them.

But the children who sat in the boat on Stallo's back caught sight of a birch that rose up above the path, and they called out to Stallo that he should go under the overhanging tree. Stallo humored them, and while he passed underneath, bent under the boat, the children lifted themselves out by holding fast to the tree. Without Stallo noticing, the boat was empty and the children gone.

Jämtland

The Sami Man Who Got Away from Stallo in a Billy Goat Skin

Stallo had no weapons or other tools, and he went around playing his flute all the time. The Sami folk could easily figure out where he was and be on their guard, but when a Sami man was out wandering, he heard some flute playing and thought, "This is a comrade!" He followed the sound and met Stallo. They began to fight right away and continued to fight until Stallo overcame the man, but in the meantime Stallo had lost an eye in the struggle.

The man was now Stallo's prisoner and could not escape him. Yet when they arrived at Stallo's home, the man hit on a plan. He began to stare keenly into the fire.

"What do you see in there?" asked Stallo.

"Ah, I see so much gold and silver," answered the man.

"I can't see that," said Stallo.

"That's because your eyes are not in good order," said the man.

"Couldn't you fix them?"

"Yes, I could, but it will be painful," said the man.

"I don't mind," said Stallo. "I can easily stand it."

So the man poured melted lead into Stallo's other eye.

Stallo was completely blind; but all the same the man could not escape because Stallo had confined him to the sheep pen. The man now took hold of Stallo's great billy goat, slaughtered it, and crept inside the skin. When the sheep were going to be taken out to graze, Stallo placed himself at the gate and let them go, one after the next, through his legs, and when the sheep had gone, the man went out on all fours inside the billy goat's skin. "Ah, it's you, my own billy goat!" said Stallo, who petted him as the man went out.

When the sheep pen was empty, Stallo went in to look for the man, who now shouted to Stallo from outside it and related how he had escaped. Stallo grew furious, and even though he couldn't see the man, he could smell well enough where he was, and he tore up a great fir tree by the roots, broke it into two pieces, and threw them after the man. But he missed, and the man was free.

Jämtland

Stallo, Who Was Tricked

Stallo once captured a Sami boy. He stuffed him in a sack, where he also had some silver coins, and then he walked on, with the sack on his back. When Stallo got tired and wanted to sleep, he released the boy and set him to collecting firewood and making a fire. The boy did as Stallo asked. He collected birch and dwarf birch and got the fire going. But he had also cut a hole at the bottom of Stallo's sack. Then the fire began to hiss, and the boy called, "The hissing fish! The hissing fish!"

When Stallo started up from his sleep, he snatched up the boy, stuffed him in the sack, and fled. But the boy and the money tumbled out of the hole in the sack. The boy shrieked, "Uh-oh, now the snake has got me." When Stallo heard what the boy shouted, he ran even faster, in his horror, without looking back. The boy remained, in possession of all the silver coins.

Margreta Bengtsson, Pite Sápmi

Stallo's Man Trap

Once Stallo made a large trap in which to catch Sami folk. At one end of an oar he mounted a bell to hear when there were people in the trap. When he was finished he took off all his clothes and lay down to sleep, but he was freezing, and so he got back up again and started a fire. The Sami, in the meantime, discovered his bell and dashed up and set it ringing without becoming trapped. Stallo ran naked from his campfire to take his expected prey. While he was gone, the Sami snuck over to Stallo's fire and tossed his clothes into the flames. After the clothes were burned, the Sami put out the fire.

When Stallo returned without his prey and saw that his clothes were burned, he cursed his own hastiness, since he believed that he himself, through carelessness and hurry, had swept his clothes into the fire. In the meantime, he built up the fire again because he was now freezing worse than before, but just as he had gotten it burning, the Sami again set off the bell. Again he had to run off, naked, in search of his catch, while the Sami again spread out the fire until it went out. When the unlucky hunter, having been fooled a second time, returned without his prey and found his fire out, he froze horribly, naked as he was. In his confusion he dashed up toward the moon, crying, "Father, your son is freezing!" The moon sucked him up and held him fast, and there he is still.

Karesuando

The Trial of Strength

Stallo was immensely strong and quite wealthy but extremely stupid. There was once a daring Sami boy who suggested a contest with Stallo. He wanted to see which of them was strongest, and the match consisted of seeing which of them could squeeze water from a stone. Stallo squeezed so hard that the stone broke into pieces and fire came out of it, but no water.

The boy had rolled a piece of watery whey cheese in sand so it looked like a stone, and he could squeeze water from "the stone."

Stallo had to admit himself beaten.

Anders Larsson, Frostviken

The Sami Man Who Married a Stallo Girl

Here in our district we've never heard anything about Stallo marrying a Sami girl, yet there is a story that a young Sami man was wed to a daughter of Stallo.

Stallo was a sort of thief. He stole reindeer from the Sami folk, and he had a large reindeer herd.

There was once a young Sami lad who hit on the idea that he should try to seduce a Stallo girl. He succeeded, and they were wed. Well, how they got married I don't know; but they probably married themselves.

The dowry was to come from Stallo, and in honor of the occasion they divided the herd so the girl could have her reindeer. Stallo had in his herd a *rabre* and a *stainak*. When they were about to separate out the girl's reindeer, the *stainak* moved constantly to the side where the girl's herd was. Stallo did not wish the *stainak* to follow that side, but the girl was so pleased to have that reindeer that Stallo finally accepted it and said, "*Gabsteb!* Let it go! It's not really gone." What he planned was to steal back the reindeer when they had been increased by the herd of his son-in-law.

The young people traveled off to the Sami lad's home. But after some time they returned to visit Stallo. They had harnessed the *stainak* to their sled; it was quick as the wind.

When they arrived at Stallo's encampment, they set up their own tent near Stallo's tent. But as the evening progressed they suspected that Stallo had evil intentions toward them. Instead of going to sleep, they dressed up a log in the clothes of the husband and put it in the sleeping area with a stone where the head should be. After that they took a sack of reindeer hair and dressed it in the wife's clothes and also placed it in the sleeping area. Now they harnessed the *stainak* and made ready to flee but remained nearby to see what would happen. In the middle of the night Stallo came with his large ax and went into the young people's tent.

There he believed he saw his daughter and son-in-law lying deep asleep. First he swung the ax at his son-in-law's head and met the stone. "The son-in-law's skull is hard!" After that he swung the ax down into the sack of reindeer hair—poof, poof, was the sound. "Now she's on her way out," said Stallo. But when he looked closer, he realized that he had been fooled. "Those little shits!" he cried angrily. So he harnessed his *rabre* and set off after them; but he couldn't catch up, because the *stainak* was faster than the *rabre*.

Stallo shouted, "*Stainak, stainak,* turn around." But the *stainak* did not stop; if it had even slightly eased its speed, Stallo would have immediately been upon them. The escapees flew behind the *stainak*; it was necessary to get over the river. On the other side of the river Stallo had no power. They got over the river on a fragile bridge of snow, and when Stallo was right behind them, trying to drive over the bridge, it broke apart under him, and Stallo drowned.

The young people now drove another route back to take the life of Stallo's wife. She had loose eyes that could be taken out and put in again. They managed to get her eyes and burned them up. They crackled in the fire, and Stallo's wife asked, "What is that crackling in the fire? I hope it's not my eyes!"

"No," said her daughter, "it was a fir branch giving off sparks."

All the same, Stallo's wife feared she was done for, and she started shouting, "Ax, ax, come and help!" At that moment the broadax came sailing through the smoke hole and met the smoke tree; it almost struck the young people, but they avoided it, barely. Afterward they killed Stallo's wife, Rutagis.

Anders Larsson, Frostviken

Stallo Eats His Grandchild

There was once a Stallo who had a daughter who married a Mountain Sami. After some time had passed, Stallo asked his son-in-law and daughter to move in with him. The Sami agreed to this and traveled to Stallo's *siida*—the fact is, he did not believe that Stallo was as dangerous as his wife said.

After they had arrived, Stallo asked if the little granddaughter could not be in the grandparents' tent at night.

"You should not take the child there," said the young wife, "because they will kill her and eat her!"

The father did not believe that, and he took the child to the grandparents' tent. But so that Stallo would not be tempted to eat the child, the young Sami slaughtered a fat reindeer, a *stainak*, and presented it to his parents-in-law.

In the evening the Sami husband went up to listen to what was happening in Stallo's tent. He heard Stallo's son say, "Give me some of the eyes of my sister's daughter."

Stallo's wife, who is called Rutagis, said, "Tomorrow you'll probably guzzle your sister's breasts and cleave your brother-in-law's marrow bones."

The Sami husband went into Stallo's tent and asked after his child.

"She's sleeping," said Stallo's wife.

The man understood what had become of his child and now asked, "When do you sleep most deeply, father-in-law?"

Stallo answered, "My deepest sleep is around midnight." Stallo always tells the truth. And now he asked, "Now, son-in-law, when do you sleep most soundly?"

The Sami answered, "It is early, as daylight comes."

Around midnight, while the Stallo family slept, the Sami husband and his wife went their way. But they took only the one tent cover with them. The other they left on the poles, so it would look as if the tent still stood there. They also left the sleeping sack lying there and put a bundle of twigs inside it, and on top of the twigs the wife placed a reindeer stomach filled with blood. The man left first; his wife was a little behind him, since she went up to the herd to fetch her *stainak* for the sled.

In the last hours of the night, Stallo went to his son-in-law's tent. With his iron spear he stabbed through the tent from the outside into the sleeping sack, where he believed the young people were sleeping. But when he pulled out the spear, there was no blood on it. He kept stabbing with his spear, until finally he hit the blood stomach, and the spear dripped with blood when he pulled it out.

Stallo cried, "Look, here you have blood for sausages from your daughter!"

And Stallo's wife answered, "Don't spill my sausage blood!"

But at the same moment, Stallo set eyes on his daughter up with the herd, where she stood with her *stainak* ready to flee when she saw what her parents were doing. Stallo ran after her, but she drove quickly away. Stallo called after her, "Wait for me, my girl!" So she eased up on her speed a little, which allowed him to take hold of the backseat of her sled; but she immediately chopped off his fingers with her ax so they fell into the sled, and after that she drove just as fast as before. Stallo cried, "Give me my fingers back!" But she drove away from him at full speed. If he had gotten his fingers back, he could have actually been able to attach them again. Stallo pursued her a long way but could not catch her.

Then the moon rose up over the top of the mountain, and Stallo cried, "There I see my father's and mother's fire!" And so he froze to death.

Margreta Bengtsson, Pite Sápmi

Russian Chudes and Other Enemies

When the Sami Lived under the Earth

In the old days, Sápmi swarmed with Russian Chudes—rough bands of thieves who plundered and murdered the Sami folk wherever they found them. The Chudes raged around mostly in summer; in winter it was too cold for them. For that reason, winter was the only time the Sami had any peace. Spring, summer, and autumn offered no safety, not for the Sami, their herds, or their belongings. So the Sami dug caves for themselves in the earth, under the roots of large trees or under the hills. They carried away the earth and sand they dug up to the lake, so it would not give them away. They also buried all their belongings. They propped up the underground tent with tree branches. There was no smoke hole; they could have a fire only at night—a tiny fire right in front of the door.

One day a party of Russian Chudes came by. One of them stayed behind to relieve himself. It was right above such an underground tent, and unluckily a little child began crying down there. The bandit heard the child and immediately figured out the connection. He struck his spear into the earth to mark the spot and went off to fetch his comrades. In the meantime the Sami had also heard him and understood well enough what would happen: the child's crying had given them away, and the bandit would return with the other Chudes to kill them. They hurried and removed the things the bandit had left, including his spear.

They carefully smoothed the spear's hole in the grass roof and erased every trace. After that they hurried back down to the tent and kept completely still.

Right afterward, the bandits returned; the Sami heard them swearing and searching. The bandit who had brought them back assured them this was the place, even though he had not found his spear. The others believed he had made fools of them, and they killed him, and then they went on their way once more.

The Sami folk now came up from the tent again, dragged the corpse away, and hid it in the willows and grasses of the bogs.

Torneträsk

The Russian Chudes between the Lakes

A *siida* consisted of three brothers, and they were *noaidis*. One night they dreamed it would go badly for them if they did not move away. Two of them immediately set off, but since the third brother did not feel like going to all the trouble of moving for the sake of a dream, he stayed.

Far away, the two *noaidis* now discovered a party of Russian Chudes between two lakes. They made themselves invisible to the bandits, and in a narrow place between the lakes they began to shoot the Chudes down with their bows and arrows. The bandits could not catch a glimpse of any enemies, and they fled, terrified, when they saw one after the next of their men falling dead on the ground. And they spread out in wild confusion on either side of the lake.

The brothers now returned to the tent to see to the third brother, but the Chudes had been there first and had killed him. If he had listened to their advice and the dream's warning, he would have survived like the others.

Karesuando

The Dreadful Ravine

Two brothers, skilled in wizardry, stood one day on a round mountain-top and watched a party of Russian Chudes coming.

One of the brothers had dreamed in the night that it would go badly with him. When it was dark, the Russian bandits lit a fire up in the ravine to have a meal and spend the night. The two Sami approached, hidden by the darkness, and thus saw that the bandits were eating with forks and that one fed the other. The Russian Chudes, in the strong glare of the fire, saw nothing out in the darkness around them. The brothers had stilled the voice of the bandits' little dog, so it could not bark and warn them. The Sami brothers now stood ready with bows and arrows. Just as one of the bandits was about to feed the captain, one of the brothers thrust the fork into the captain's mouth so it went down his throat, and at the same moment the other brother shot an arrow at them. The Chudes, who believed the worst of each other, now began to fight among themselves. The Sami brothers observed the battle from a distance, shooting at them all the while, until every one of the Chudes was killed. When the bandits were dead, one of the brothers walked over to see them. He was the one who had had the bad dream during the night. His brother warned him against it, but he did not obey. When he came to where the Chudes lay, there was still enough life in one of them that the bandit was able to draw his sword and hack the Sami in the heel so he died.

Karesuando

The Russian Chudes Who Drove Headless

A party of Russian Chudes was out robbing near Lake Inari. During the night one of them dreamed that they departed the lake, strangely without their heads. "That is surely a bad dream," said one of them, yet they continued on their robbing expedition to Inari.

They went first to two Sami brothers who lived together. When the brothers saw the Russian Chudes coming, they had to figure out what to do. Now, the two Sami had a reindeer particularly good for driving, which always went just where it should. They did not want the reindeer to go to the Russian Chudes; for that reason they singed off the reindeer's hair, so it would look ugly.

Meanwhile, the Russian Chudes came and they appeared friendly. They asked the brothers to guide them over the frozen lake to the town. The Sami men promised to do this, and so that the Russian Chudes would not freeze, they were packed into the sleds and tied down well. There was a heavy snow fog when the brothers drove off with them.

One of the brothers drove in front and the other last, such that they had the Russian Chudes in a long string of sleds between them. The brother in back had taken the fast reindeer, and he now raced forward alongside the Chudes and chopped off their heads, one after the next, with an ax. One of the Chudes in front turned around and looked back, and when he saw his comrade behind driving without his head, he thought, "Well, he's probably driving so fast that he's lost his hat on the ice."

The brother managed to chop the head off the last Russian Chude, and so they survived that time.

Anni Rasti, Karesuando

The Legend of the Seven Sleepers

Some Christian people were pursued by Chudes, who wanted to kill them. They sought refuge in a cave and lay down to sleep. Right after they had gone into the cave, a spider came along and wove its web over the cave's entrance. When the pursuers arrived and saw the spun web, they thought that no one could have gone into the cave recently. They gave up their pursuit and lay down to sleep in another cave.

The Christian folk slept for three hundred years before they woke up. They walked down to the closest town, which was Tromsø. It had become much larger than before. When they first went to sleep there was only one merchant; now there were many. They could not recognize the town at all, and their money had grown so old that no one would accept it.

Then they understood they had slept for three hundred years.

Later they went back up to see what had become of their pursuers, who had gone to sleep in another cave. All that remained of them was a little dust.

Jouna Rasti, Karesuando

The Blind Old Woman

In a Sami *siida* there was a blind old woman. She was tired of never knowing what other people laughed about. She could not see when anything funny went on. But she asked others to give her a shove when anything comic happened, so that she could laugh with the others.

One day, the Sami folk heard the bandits coming, and everyone fled. Only the old woman remained behind.

The bandits had a Sami man as a guide, and as they swarmed now into the tent, they ended up shoving the woman, and she began to laugh loudly in the belief that something was happening that was especially funny. The bandits were surprised and asked why the woman was laughing like that. The Sami guide quickly answered, "Well, you see that she is an old witch, who is right in the midst of practicing her skills." Hearing that, the bandits became so terrified that they ran away. In that way the blind old woman saved the whole *siida*.

Västerbotten

The Headland of the Murdered

One evening during the time when the Sami folk lived underground, an old woman went outside. She heard noise and said quite loudly, "Hear how the sea roars!" She believed it was the sea that thundered, but it was the thundering Russian Chudes, who broke the peace of the night with their noise.

The Chudes heard the old woman's outburst, and because of that the Sami settlement was robbed. The Chudes attacked them and there was a great battle and din because of an unusually large number of Sami folk in the *siida*. But the Russian Chudes killed every one of them. Since then the place has been called Olbmugoddemnjargga, the headland of the murdered. You can still find kettles and tools at the site; the place is badly haunted and frightens people who go by it.

Karesuando

The Russian Chudes Who Were Blown Up

A band of Chudes came one evening to a Sami *siida*, where everyone had fled except an old woman. She hung the stewpot over the fire and gave the bandits a hearty meal of meat. When they had eaten and were very tired, she bade them lie down to sleep securely: she would stay awake and guard them. After they were all asleep, she stole their powder horns and emptied the powder from all the horns into a bowl. Then she went out and tied the tent door open. She then threw the powder on the fire while she ran out of the way. The whole tent exploded, and all the bandits died.

Västerbotten

The Sami Man Who Created a Storm

Once, during the "Thirty Years' War," a robber band came rowing up the Strømsvattu Valley, and a neighbor of a Sami man, my grandfather's grandfather Ballo Lars, came to him and said, "Now we're going to die, all of us. A robber band is rowing over the lake to us and will kill us!" "No," answered Ballo Lars, "they surely won't, and you farmers can also be calm." The Sami took his old ax and went up to a huge mountain and

The Sami took his old ax and went up to a huge mountain and hacked at the stones.

hacked at the stones. It was sunny and clear, but now one cloud after the next began to arise, until the heavens were dark and a terrible storm with thunder and lightning came up, so that all the robbers drowned.

The place where it happened can still be seen.

Märta Nilsson, Jämtland

The Sami Girls Who Escaped the Bandits

In the Harkel Mountains two bandits attacked a girl herding reindeer. It was Pål Fredriksson's mother, when she was young. They took the brass ring that hangs from the belt of all Sami women, with its scissors and knife and sewing tools, and then they took off her clothes, all except her trousers. Afterward they put her between them, since they wanted to sleep. So that she wouldn't escape they each took one of her braids and wrapped it fast around their arms. Other than that, they didn't harm her. The plan was that she would show them the storehouse when it grew light, after they'd had some sleep.

Meanwhile, they slept so heavily that she managed to steal back her knife. She cut off her braids and jumped up. Just then the two robbers woke and set out after her. So she ran over a "sink bog," which could only bear her weight, since she knew where to put her feet. But the robbers sank into it and couldn't get any farther. Half-naked as she was, she dashed home to the tent, and there she pulled some clothes out from under the tent cover and put them on.

Another girl was attacked in the same way by such a bandit, but she managed to get hold of her scissors, and she stabbed both points in his eye. In this amazing way, she escaped from him.

Märta Nilsson, Jämtland

The Sami Girls Who Stirred Up a Snowstorm

The Chudes came once to a rich widow who had a great reindeer herd and two daughters. The bandits took the girls and the herd. The girls were supposed to keep watch over the reindeer for them and show them the way to other *siidas*.

As they were taken away, their mother gave her daughters a bag of feathers and good advice. She was in fact a woman wise in sorcery.

In the evening, when the Chudes and the girls had set up the tent to spend the night, the bandits undressed and lay down to sleep, while the girls went out to guard the reindeer against the wolves. They asked the Chudes to come if they cried for help, because that meant that the wolves were among the reindeer. They promised to do so, and the girls left. When they had been out a short while, they called for help and at the same time unloosed the bag of feathers. Right away a furious snowstorm blew up, and the Chudes, who hastened to help the girls, were lost in the storm and perished. After that the girls drove the reindeer herd home to their mother.

Karesuando

"The South Wind Bangs against Bird Mountain"

One day a group of Russian Chudes came whizzing on skis down from a mountainside. The snow had a springtime crust, and so it sounded like a wailing wind when the skiers advanced. In the tent sat the Sami, and they shouted, "The south wind bangs against Bird Mountain." But they soon realized it was the Chudes on their way. A girl was curious and peeked out the door, but as her parents pulled on her from the inside and the Chudes from the outside, they tore the girl in two. After that the Chudes broke in and killed all the Sami in the tent.

Karesuando

The King Believed That the Sami Were Animals

The Sami do not believe it was only the Russian Chudes who plagued them in olden times; no, it was also the Finns! The Finns considered the Sami to be wild animals and killed them like dogs, like swine, and treated them according to their pleasure. The Sami were not registered in the king's census. The king lives far to the south. He had been made to believe that the Sami were not human, and he, who was so far away, could not know this was a lie.

But there was a merchant in Karesuando who was sympathetic toward the Sami. This merchant managed to have a Sami man by the name of Labba—his descendants are still alive—sent down to the king in a packing case. He had to be sent in a packing case so that he would not be seen underway and killed. And this allowed him to ask the king whether he was a human being or an animal. The king said then that the Sami were people like other people, and he arranged for laws to be made so that no one had permission to kill them and treat them like animals. Since that time the Sami have been registered in the king's census.

Anni Rasti, Karesuando

The Sami Man Who Tricked the Enemies and Saved the Farmers

During the time when there were bandits afoot in Sweden, a party of them met a Sami man and demanded that he guide them to a farming hamlet. He guided them around and around the whole day without arriving at the hamlet, and when evening came, he lit a bark torch and walked in front of them with this light. The Sami guide now brought them to a mountain where boulders tumbled down the steep slope. Here he threw his torch down to the bottom, and it bumped from stone to stone, so the bandits believed that the guide had started to run down the slope, and they followed him, but all of them fell and were killed.

The Sami man crept down to where he had thrown the torch, and now he went to the hamlet. There was a wedding taking place, and the guests, as was their custom, began immediately to mock and make fun of him. But the Sami man told them they shouldn't mock him; if it hadn't been for his saving their lives this evening they would have all been death's children. The next morning he guided them out to the mountain slope, and when they saw all their enemies lying dead there, they no longer ridiculed the Sami man but thanked him because he had saved their lives.

Jonas Persson, Härjedalen

How the Sami in the Hotag Mountains Killed the Enemies

During the time of unrest in Sweden when the robber bands roamed around, a group of them came up to the Hotag Mountains. Two Sami families lived there at the time. A deep valley or pass went between two steep mountains, through which the robbers were to travel. The Sami placed all their sleds on one mountainside, filled them with stones and reindeer antlers, and then tied them all together. When their enemies came through the pass, the Sami pushed the whole thing over, so all the strangers were crushed, and the Sami were saved that time.

Jonas Persson, Härjedalen

Tju'jaure

The legend says that in the old days the Sami here in the south of Sweden were gradually wiped out by the farmers and bandits. The strain of wild reindeer found here earlier was nothing more than abandoned tame reindeer that had spread out after their owners died.

Many years ago, it's told, there were only two farming families in Ljusnedal, and up in the mountains lived some Sami folk. One of the Sami families had a deaf-mute son, and he had a sort of vision. He foretold that the farmers had evil intentions. They wanted to murder the Sami, and because of that the Sami should quickly move away to another place, both people and reindeer. So the deaf-mute's family moved away, but the others trusted the farmers too well. They stayed where they were.

The Sami who stayed were very rich, with several thousand reindeer. They had three children: a grown daughter, a younger boy who was an uncommonly fast runner, and then a little baby, who still lay in the cradle. The boy was the godson of a farmer's wife in Ljusnedal, and she had told him that if anything happened to them, he should run to her right away (what the farmers, in fact, feared was that when the crime took place the fast-running boy might escape and run for help somewhere else). The farmers had gotten information in advance from the young Sami lad about where the father and the others in the tent had their bedding.

So, one night the farmers set off—others say that the crime occurred in the middle of the day, a bright summer day. They first encountered the Sami daughter herding the reindeer at night out on a headland. They spoke in a friendly way to the girl and gave her food they had brought along, as they bade her keep the reindeer here on the headland until they returned for their sack of food. She suspected nothing wrong, remained there with the reindeer, ate the food, and thought that these were kind people who came and gave her food during the night watch.

The farmers walked on, and when they came to the tent that lay in the dense thicket, they began to clear away the juniper bushes and trees, so that nothing should stand in their way later. The woman in the tent heard the farmers making their way there and said to her husband, "Why in the world would they clear the brush?"

"Oh, it's probably so it will look nicer here," answered the man—he was not suspicious.

But at the same moment, the farmers broke into the tent and killed them all. And when they lifted up the cloth covering the baby, who hung in its cradle next to its mother, the baby smiled at them; but they took it by its legs and banged its head against one of the stones by the door, so it died.

The boy, who was so skilled at running, had crept out of the tent in all the confusion, and now he ran to his godmother's farm. After the farmers had killed the Sami they wanted to kill the reindeer, and so they returned to the girl who was herding. When they had gotten her to drive the reindeer all the way out on the headland, they tied a stone around her neck and drowned her in the lake. It is now called Tju'jaure, but the farmers call it Ögonsjön, or Lake of the Eyes.

They slaughtered as many of the reindeer as they could get their hands on. The rest of the herd grew so terrified by the smell of blood that they threw themselves in the lake and swam away. They spread out in the mountains and became wild reindeer.

When the farmers returned home in the morning, the boy shouted, as soon as he saw them in the farmyard, "Here come the bad people!"

"Oh, *tull*," said the farmwife. "They are just our people."

The child understood now what had happened and fled as fast as his legs could carry him; but the farmers pursued the boy, and as he was about to jump over a creek, his belt snapped and his trousers fell, so he could not run, and now the farmers grabbed the boy and killed him too. Since then the creek is called Murder Creek; the farmers call it Finn Creek.

But know this, everything came out in the end, because the pastor at Storsjøen noticed that the Sami folk no longer came to the services on holy days, and he grew suspicious of the farmers. The case was reported, and the provincial governor came, and his wife came with him. The governor got the whole story from the farmers by pretending that he was on the farmers' side and by saying that they should think about finishing off the Sami. Then they said that it had already been done, and they told the story of how it had happened. But when they had told about the little baby in the cradle, who smiled as they picked it up, the governor's wife cried, "No, I can't stand to hear any more, dear husband, you must jail them!"

Elisabet Rensberg, Härjedalen

When the Farmers Wanted to Stamp Out the Sami

In my grandfather's time, the farmers in Ljungdalen decided that all the Sami in Ljungdalen, Mittådalen, Grönvallen, and Skärvagsdalen should be killed. They wrote to a farmer in Bruksvallarna that he should kill the Sami in Grönvallen, but he wrote back that he would not go along with murdering the Sami and no servant from his farm would go along with such a thing. The rumor of the farmers' scheme leaked out among the Sami; and my grandfather, who expected that he would soon die, went to the pastor in Handöl chapel—he was the pastor in Undersåker—and asked him for the last rites. It was on a Saturday, and the pastor believed he was drunk, so he asked my grandfather to come another day. The day afterward, Sunday morning, he came again and asked to be given last rites. The pastor asked what he meant by this, and my grandfather told him that the farmers had decided to kill all the Sami. "Dear Renander," said the pastor, "that will never happen." The pastor saw to it that the sheriff made his way to Ljungdalen and stopped the farmers' scheme.

A farmer's wife later said to my grandfather, "Yes, now you'll be allowed to live, since the Lapp King (the sheriff) has been here."

The farmers were also given to frightening the Sami. My father told me that one of the farmer neighbors stayed up a whole night throwing stones at the tent. But that same night a wolf ate all the farmer's sheep.

Elisabet Rensberg, Härjedalen

The Disguised Farmers

In my parents' time the Sami were still afraid of wandering folk and of farmers. The farmers could disguise themselves as gypsies and try to rob and steal from the Sami. My uncle was once on his way to his storage hut with reindeer cheese, which was tied onto the pack reindeer. The storage hut was in a hidden spot in the forest.

As he was walking, he was followed by his own farmer neighbors, although he didn't recognize them in their disguises. He tied up the reindeer in a birch forest and cut himself a birch switch for self-defense and turned to his pursuers. He hit them hard on their hands, so they lost their knives and fled.

He did not recognize them on that occasion, but when he later met his neighbors, he saw that they had bruises on their hands.

Elisabet Rensberg, Härjedalen

Karin Wildstar

In the old days there was a pastor in Hede or Ljusnedal who, along with the sheriff and district governor, had decided to drive out the Sami. The pastor had therefore written a false letter from the king about how the Sami should be murdered. He wanted to read this letter in church, and on one of the holy days he asked the Sami to gather together so he could read the king's proclamation to them.

But you shall hear, there was a brave Sami woman with three children. Like the others, she had heard rumors of what the letter contained. She went with her husband that Sunday to the church and went into the rectory before the service. She saw that there, on the desk of the pastor, lay a pile of papers he had set out to take into the church with him, and among them was the king's letter. Just as the Sami woman came in, a strange gentleman drove up to the rectory, and the pastor went out to receive him.

The Sami woman then snapped up the document and shoved it down into her trousers. Some of the other papers she threw on the fire, and the pastor's children, who were wandering around the room, took some papers too and tossed them on the fire.

While the pastor was receiving the strange gentleman, she sneaked away. Afterward she put her three children in a sled and drove off. The Sami woman wanted to go to Stockholm and talk with the king. "It is the same to me whether I am killed at the king's palace or here in the mountains."

So she set off on her way down to Idre through Dalarna and then on to Stockholm.

She had put on her new fur coat, and all the children were in new fur coats. When Karin arrived just outside Stockholm, she met a gentleman—it was the king, but he didn't reveal himself. He spoke with her and marveled at their appearance, wondering whether they were people or animals, and he was also amazed that they were to be found in his kingdom. Then he asked her straight out what she wanted here. Well, she wanted to meet the king, and she asked the way. The king took out a piece of paper and wrote something on it. He gave it to the Sami woman, while telling her that she should show the paper when she came into the city. She did this, and on the paper it was written what time the next day she should meet the king. She was to be given lodging for the night.

The next day, when Karin appeared before the king, she called out in Jesus's name to ask if it was true that she and her people were to be exterminated. The king said no, but now the Sami woman produced the letter that she had taken from the pastor's desk. The king looked at it and immediately said it was a false letter. The king now asked what her name was. She said Karin. "Hereafter you shall be called Karin Wildstar!" said the king.

Yes, we heard a lot about Karin Wildstar, but that was in the old days.

All the others, the district governor, the pastor, and the sheriff, took their own lives, because they feared the violent punishment that would be meted out to them. Yes, if there had been no Karin Wildstar, there would be no Sami in Härjedalen today either.

Elisabet Rensberg, Härjedalen

Nuelesgiete

The Nuelesgiete were a sort of Sami folk who were said to live far to the north in Sápmi, where the main branch of the Sami have their home—we are only a small group that has wandered down from the north.

Nuelesgiete spoke pure Sami; the language we speak down here is a "wild language." Nuelesgiete are said to have lived in tents under the earth and to have used bows and arrows, a kind of weapon that other people must not know about and use. This weapon was called *nueleske,* and no other people had its like.

It is the Nuelesgiete who hold us up, and they appear at times to see if we are alive. It's only men who appear, and they journey at whatever time of day they please and as fast as they please. They can walk around invisibly, and they can do both good and evil. It is impossible to catch them. The farmers could not get the better of them; they were more likely to kill the farmers.

All the Sami believed in earlier times that they existed and that they traveled around the mountains and paid attention to how things went with the Sami down south and that they revenged wrongs against the Sami. But it was hard to hold your own when you met the Nuelesgiete. It was difficult to know how you should behave, when you should eat— what you should take first and which pieces. For example, you should eat the fat first; if you did not do that, they would kill you.

Lisbet, an old Sami woman, said that she did not know much about the Nuelesgiete; she had never spoken with them. But once, when she was herding the reindeer in springtime, she glimpsed a strange Sami man who walked among the reindeer. He was tall and wore a fine, soft fur. He walked with his arms crossed over his chest under the fur and inspected the herd and peered at their earmarks. Lisbeth went toward him and called to him, but he did not answer, and when she came over, he was gone. She searched for his footprints, but there were none.

When the other reindeer herders came to relieve her, she asked if a stranger had come to the *siida*, "because a gentleman walked through the herd wearing such a fine cap." But they made fun of her, because she went around saying such "foolish things."

"Of course it was a Nuelesgiete who was inspecting the herd," she said, and she added, "Nuelesgiete are dangerous and evil, they eat the heart out of a person, and you don't know anything of it before a little blood is seen around the mouth."

Lisbet Nilsdotter, Jämtland

Field Notes and Commentary

Material in brackets is written by the translator or is from Emilie Demant Hatt's glossary in the original Danish edition of *By the Fire*.

Moose, Lucky Reindeer, Reindeer Luck, and Wizardry

Legends about moose are distributed most widely in the southern Lap-marks (Härjedalen and Jämtland), where they are commonly known everywhere. Among the Northern Sami we have encountered only hints of legends about tame moose.

"The Sun's Daughter with the Tame Moose Herd"

[This story from Ottfjället, a small Sami settlement in northern Jämtland, was told to Demant Hatt by Marja Maria Nilsson, the half sister of Morten Thomasson, with whom the Hatts spent some days in September 1912. Demant Hatt writes in her field notes from that year that she heard several stories about moose in Ottfjället and farther north, in Undersåker. In her glossary Demant Hatt defines *boassjo (boaššo)* as "the area of the tent farthest from the door, where food and cooking gear is stowed. In the old days it was the holiest part of the tent, where no one should step, in any case not the women, who were seen by the Sami, as by so many in-digenous people, as unclean."—Trans.]

"How the Sami Were Given Reindeer and Tents by the Underground Folk and How the Settlers Were Given Farms and Farm Animals"

The underground folk play a great role in the imaginations of the Sami. Sami ideas about them are not so different from Scandinavian beliefs in underground folk: giants, elves, trolls, Huldras, roe deer, and so forth. This little tale is unusual in having the character of an origin story, as it shows how the Sami have imagined how their nomad life began, while their neighbors received farms and domestic animals and started to till the land. [In *By the Fire* Demant Hatt speaks of Haldes as synonymous with Uldas, both Sami terms that mean underground folk. In earlier times a Halde (*háldejaš*) was a guardian spirit of a natural place, for instance, a spring or river, but the two concepts have merged. The Huldra or Hulder is a forest spirit, generally a female, often a temptress, in Scandinavian folk literature.—Trans.]

The tale was recorded in Pite Sápmi in 1916 [1914], and we haven't encountered it in other places in this form, despite the common, widespread belief among all Sami that they, on various occasions, were given reindeer from the underground folk. The reindeer obtained in this mystic way are always beautiful and strong; they are likely to be white or white spotted, something the Sami value highly.

That the Sami neither "swear nor joke" when they are milking the reindeer is, to this day, quite correct. When the herd is gathered, either in the corral or on the patches of snow, for milking or earmarking, or when the herd is gathered to separate out the pack reindeer or animals to be slaughtered or to separate out other people's reindeer that have become mixed up in the herd, then the work is undertaken with as little noise as possible and completely without coarse and harsh words. Certainly, in other circumstances, oaths and swearing are well known among the Sami. Yet bystanders don't enjoy such oaths but condemn them as being less than harmless invocations to the Evil One. [As Demant Hatt mentions in her Introduction, *norrose i gorose* is a nonsense phrase in Sami, which is nevertheless always included in the telling of this story.—Trans.]

"The Old Woman Who Made Reindeer Herding Difficult" was recorded among the Karesuando Sami, but we have a similar version from the Sami of Jämtland.

"The Sami Lad Who Married a Halde Girl and Was Given Lucky Reindeer Along with Her"

Certain reindeer in the herd—or a single reindeer—are viewed as particularly lucky, and through inheritance or dowry, one is naturally very eager to come into possession of such animals. The tale was recorded among the Karesuando Sami in 1916.

[*Siida* is an age-old Sami word meaning community, often composed of related families; in *By the Fire* Demant Hatt generally uses it to describe a nomadic or seminomadic tent community.—Trans.]

The pictures: The intent is to show a summer night in a Norwegian mountain area. The Sami is stepping—after a disturbing night's sleep—from the tent, a small, low, grass-roofed hut. He asks the weeping girl to come into the tent. She belongs to him now and can no longer return to her own family. Her friend, on the other hand, goes back to where she came from. Up near the tent the dog has stationed itself, partly to doze a little, partly to have a view of the reindeer. The dog understands that the people down there are far too absorbed in their own affairs to think about the reindeer, for which it feels full responsibility.

The next image doesn't need much explanation: at sunset there's a happy journey heading to the freedom of the mountains. At the front the reindeer herd moves at speed, held together by the eager dog and followed by the owner with his lasso and reins over his shoulder. After him comes his young wife, who has given him happiness and lucky reindeer. She leads a string of reindeer that carry their remaining possessions.

"How the Sami Girl Tricked the Evil One" and the following story were recorded in 1908 among the Karesuando Sami. There are many legends among the Sami, both in the north and in the south, of selling one's soul to an evil spirit—or, following the usual fairy-tale formula, to the Devil, Bærgalak. But the things the Sami want to obtain by sacrificing either themselves or a child or something valuable are always the same: reindeer luck, the herd's welfare. Money is not the Sami's standard of value, but reindeer, reindeer! The sight of the great living herd, when it comes clattering over the mountains, is what warms the Sami's heart above all else. And the happiness of owning this magnificence is so great and so desirable that one can sacrifice his own soul or even that of his own child to gain it.

In the old days, when the Sami sacrificed to their gods large and small gifts, as their intellect and abilities afforded, there was always the wish: reindeer luck!

The notion of lucky reindeer is widespread in the Lapmarks. The *stainak* also belongs to this category. Sometimes among the Sami's tame reindeer one finds a curious reindeer cow that never calves. This is called a *stainak*. She is larger and more beautiful than the normal *aldo*; her antlers are powerful, many branched, sitting on her head like a crown. She is strong and runs "like lightning," and she has a lot of stamina when running. A *stainak* is the leader of the herd: she runs at its head, she brings luck, she is thought to be connected to the supernatural, and her splendid qualities are known and treasured from north to south in the whole of Lapland. A *stainak* is slaughtered as rarely as possible; she is allowed to live out her days, but if a *stainak* comes home of her own free will and places herself at the slaughtering place behind the tent, it means that—in times past—she should be killed. A sacrifice is required for the welfare of the herd, for the Sami's good fortune.

A Sami man told the story of how his paternal aunt had a *stainak*, fifteen years old. "Last year" the *stainak* died. She ran off, fourteen or fifteen miles, but came back to her herd and died on her own. The aunt was happy about the good fortune that the *stainak* died at home: "the spirits returned with her." [These are 15 Swedish miles, or around 150 kilometers or 93 American miles.—Trans.]

The Sami continued: "But now it is rare that one hears about the *stainak*, perhaps because in our time one doesn't have such good knowledge of the herd. But it is hardly more than five years ago that a Sami man drove to Arjeplog with a *stainak* pulling his sled." An animal with similar characteristics is a *rabre*, a reindeer cow who doesn't calve. We could not get a clear understanding of the difference between a *stainak* and a *rabre*.

"*Stainak* and the Sami Man Who Died" was recorded in the most northern part of Jämtland in Frostviken, near the border with Västerbotten. It is, like all the stories, reproduced as literally as possible. It needs no explanation, since the storyteller gives the necessary information for understanding the story.

The image illustrates the moment when the herder has brought the reindeer back to the corral, right around sunrise, and now finds the Sami lying dead in the corral on the slope of the enclosure. The reindeer stand quietly resting, while the dog keeps an eye on the remaining animals that haven't entered the corral with the herd. The herder has his staff in his left hand; he has on a rain cape and a lasso over his back.

"The Sami Man Who Wanted His Dead Wife Back" was recorded in same place as the previous story [Frostviken, 1913]. That a Sami shaman, a *noaidi*, could perform both good and evil with regard to the dead and visit them in their kingdom is seen as settled fact. The failure to bring the beloved wife back in this case is due to the circumstance that the man's two herders were not quite ignorant of the arts of sorcery insofar as they understood they had to be on their guard. If they had followed the order to untie the corpse of the dead woman at the moment she showed a sign of life by lifting her hand in the air, then one of them would have been taken in place of the corpse, which naturally enough neither of them wanted to happen. They both ran away in the decisive moment. This put the Sami man down in the kingdom of the dead in great danger. He can get his wife back only by offering another soul, and when that fails, the spirits attack him, so he can only barely escape back to life again.

In the picture the corpse lies tied down in a sled up on a *site,* a high platform that the Sami traditionally use to protect the dead against wild animals and dogs until a burial can take place. [Demant Hatt's use of the word *site* in her story text and in this note is probably a variant of the Sami word *siedi,* or shrine.–Trans.]

"The Reindeer-Herding Ghost" and "The Shoes Sewn from Human Skin"
These two stories tell the same thing: *noaidis* have the power to bind the spirits to their service. The shoes from the churchyard most probably can be regarded as a spirit that, at the *noaidi's* command, forces the farmhand to serve his master, as long as he obeys the ban against wearing them to church. The first of these stories was recorded among the Karesuando Sami in 1908 and the second in 1912 among the Härjedalen Sami.

"The Wizardly Sami Girl" was recorded among the Karesuando Sami in 1916 and likely doesn't need any explanation about why the girl becomes angry because her mother has treated the two other girls to coffee. If a man comes to a tent on an errand of courtship, or is "sounding things out" to see if the mood is favorable to his plans, then it is a good sign and almost a promise if he is offered coffee. And the daughter therefore becomes angry at her mother, because she has invited the two girls. The daughter doesn't want them in the family since they are quarrelsome and poor, and she demonstrates this by turning them into goats. A stubborn and intemperate disposition is in general resented in Sami circles, where life is lived more openly in front of the eyes and ears of family and neighbors. Nor does anyone like to expose oneself to gossip through a marriage partner's ungoverned words and actions. When an intemperate disposition is coupled with poverty, one understands that such a person is not desirable as a tent mate or family member. The word "poor" has a very loose meaning among the Sami. One can be poor even if one is rich in reindeer or money. If one is sickly, is disabled, or has other sorrows or hardships that pursue one in life, and if one is unlucky, without good friends or friendly kinfolk, then one is "poor."

Sickness Spirits

"The Sickness Spirit That Arrived on a Stick of Wood" and "The Sickness Spirits That Froze in the High Mountains"

These two stories were recorded in northern Frostviken.

That sickness is brought about by sickness spirits is a familiar concept among the Sami, from south to north. Typically these spirits are thought to keep mainly to farming villages or to closely populated places. If someone has been down "in the village," he can be unlucky enough to get a sickness spirit in the hairs of his fur clothing and in this way carry it with him to the high mountains. Here the spirit, naturally enough, freezes and doesn't thrive. This first story shows there is a reason to respect old ways and customs. The firewood pile should be neatly placed inside the door, which should be closed, since outside, especially at twilight, the dead and the sickness spirits wander about, and through the door everything evil can come in. "Sickness spirits are just devils that wander under the sun," added the storyteller.

The illustration to the first story shows the interior of a Sami tent in the evening. The large stewpot hangs steaming over the fire. The coffee kettle, always on hand, is on one of the hearthstones in front of the man to the left. Over his head, on one of the tent's cross poles, hangs a pair of gloves. The stranger had been sitting down in the usual place for guests, just inside the door. Now he has gotten up and swings the ax toward the sickness spirit, which is not visible but, like the man, sits in front of the housewife. The two old people in the tent don't understand the guest's behavior; the housewife raises her hands to her head, terrified, as if to ward off the blow. To her right can be seen a bit of the little Sami chest, one of the small oval boxes in which the Sami keep their valuables: money, psalmbooks, silk ribbons, pipes, and so on. The old father to the left reaches over the fire, as if to hinder the guest from using the ax in this inexplicable way. The dog, which pokes its head out in the far bottom left, is also full of amazement over what is happening. But the "steel ax" demonstrates its devastating effect on evil. One can well imagine that the poor Sami man gets both a dressing down and outpourings of gratitude when, after a deed executed so opportunely, he explains his actions.

The second story has many variants. The smallpox lies in the cleft of the mountain rock, freezing, and pleads pitifully with passing Sami folk to be carried down again, so it will "never again come up here to the high mountains."

It also happens that the pestilence lies in a crowded street, in the shape of a silk ribbon or something similar that a Sami man picks up and carries away until he has an unpleasant suspicion about what he might be carrying. He throws the fine object away up on the bare mountainside, and ever since then the plague lies there whining and begging to be borne down to a warmer place.

"The Sami Woman Who Saw Fever and Another Sickness Spirit" was recorded in Härjedalen, and its ending closely resembles the way of thinking of the two previous stories.

Murdered Children

That infanticide can occur among the Sami, as well as among other kinds of people, is self-evident, but these and similar stories show how risky such actions are, even if they never come to the knowledge of others or are punished under the law. A child murdered and left exposed cries and cries and reveals the crime. One can seek to hinder this by different methods, for example, in the first story with the scissors, which seems particularly awful. The punishment doesn't materialize at the time either. The first image shows the young mother's fear when she finally has found the corpse in the eerie, dark stone scree. She has seized her scissors, and at the same moment the specter grows before her eyes and reaches for the scissors, the instrument of torture with which the hard-hearted mother murdered her baby.

After that comes the journey to the father at home in the tent. But when the specter [the *epper*] arrives in the *siida*, it looks for its relatives and goes into its aunt's tent. She demonstrates extraordinary courage and understanding of the situation by offering the ghostly child baptism in the bathwater of its living cousin. Baptism (admission into the society of the living and the dead) is exactly what such an outlaw soul craves. Among the older Sami this bathwater was viewed as holy. It was blessed with the sign of the cross, with steel, with glowing coals or the like, and it wasn't to be tossed out in any old place after use.

In Pite Sápmi it was supposed to be poured out under "the master's stone." In this region, many of the hearthstones are named after different members of the family since they are set out around the fire where different people sit. In the picture one sees the tent interior at nightfall; in the foreground is the warm campfire with the coffee kettle in its place. Next to this sits "Aunt" with her child; behind the large brass or copper kettle, where the bathing happens, is the cradle ready for the little one's night sleep. Just inside the door the dead child can be seen in conversation with his warm-hearted and brave aunt.

In the story it's told that the murdered child who came to life again "had an especially large head," that his aunt had not "formed" it "when she bathed him." This alludes to the fact that in earlier times the Sami formed children's heads with gentle pressing, with firm bindings and tightly fitting caps. This massage, which took place in connection with bathing when the infant was quite small, could also be extended to the throat, arms, and legs, but it was mostly the head that was "formed." This was done to close the fontanel more quickly and with an intention to beautify. A small, round head belonged to the Sami conception of beauty.

Animals

Stories about dogs were recorded in Pite Sápmi and don't really need explanation, only a couple of clarifying comments.

The wolverine "broke open a *gisa* and ate everything in it": a *gisa* is a large limb from a birch tree, bent to form an oval; its bottom and lid consist of loops of rope or tendon, which are tied around meat or other things packed in birch bark. In such *gisas* the Sami transport their belongings when they migrate. A pair of *gisas* is connected with loops and hangs equally balanced over the sides of the pack reindeer.

Including the detail that the Sami woman was afraid that the dog would want too great a wage is quite significant and psychologically accurate. A suggestion of something similar is found in Turi's variation from the Northern Sami, where the Sami also asks what the dog would like to be paid for his work. ["The Dog Was Once a Wild Animal," in *An Account of the Sámi.*—Trans.] By all accounts from the Sami in the north and south, the "ancient Sami" were very stingy; the servants, children, and dogs went hungry. The Sami of olden times did not have the heart to slaughter the reindeer in sufficiently large numbers to provide for their families, servants, and dogs—naturally the dogs had it the worst. That the circumstances were such seems clear from this old saying, which contains a warning: "If you yourself eat and don't give the children and dogs anything, then you break your child's heart and your dog's spirit."

That the dog prefers "soup and bones" as its payment is a very humble request. The Sami most often eat boiled reindeer meat, and the strong broth that results is something they can't finish off, nor can the soup be preserved for later use. They prepare dog food with dried reindeer blood and a little flour. The dog is usually given only the ribs and shoulder blades. Mainly for religion reasons you did not give the rest of the reindeer bones to the dogs.

"The Bear That Carried Jesus over the River" is a well-known animal fable in the southern Lapmarks and Västerbotten as well as in Pite Sápmi. It is only recalled in pieces. The best version we have was recorded in Pite Sápmi.

"The Loon"

The tale of the loon is known in all the Swedish Lapmarks from north to south; its remarkable scream, strange shape, and sharp beak have awakened the imagination and inspired the idea that it is an enchanted and magic bird. It is a bad omen to hear its scream when one has not eaten. The beak was used by the Sami sorcerers of old as an arrowhead, since it could not be bewitched. The loon always sacrifices three eggs to the sea, on whose surface it has its nest. The story was recorded in Pite Sápmi. The first episode, about the loon's feet, is also known in the northern Lapmarks. About the origin of the loon's unpleasant voice we have, in addition to this version from Pite Sápmi, a second one from Härjedalen: The loon had its nest on a small island. A Sami man took his clothes off and swam out to the island to gather the eggs, but the loon dived down and stabbed the man with its sharp beak right in the heart, so he died. At the same moment, the Sami man screamed—and the loon has had this death scream ever since.

"Origins of Lice"

Pite Sápmi. Similar versions are also known in the other Lapmarks.

"Snake Cure"

[In her glossary, Demant Hatt offers this long definition of the *joik:* "Joiking is the Sami's particular form of song, half-recited, half-sung, expressing the mood of the moment. They create the words and melody themselves, as it strikes them, or they use old words and melodies. In earlier times joiking played an extremely large role. The Sami joiked on all occasions, both when alone and when together with others. Each child received his or her own 'song,' a little melody with a short text, three or four notes, three or four words, like a joik always is. But the joik can be drawn out and repeated as wished. This little personal song given to a child is something they keep their entire life, and later they might inherit several more, some praising and some mocking. When such a personal joik is performed, you immediately know the person in mind. These short songs can contain the finest poetry; at the same time people can joik about ordinary things, and they can joik with evil or threatening intent. The joik offers a shifting expression for everything in a Sami person's life: people, relationships, reindeer, stars, snow, wild animals, hate, love, and motherly tenderness—everything that moves through the mind of a Sami individual and before their eyes. But this special poetic art of the Sami, the joik, is diminished and hated by pastors and missionaries, who with fanatic eagerness have made the Sami imagine that their old song art was a great sin, which could take them straight to Hell. In all honesty I must add that there are now among some of the younger minds signs of understanding the Sami's ancient culture in this way as well. But no one can repair the harm done; the older generation has been convinced that joiking is sinful. They can't stand to hear it in the tents, and thus naturally the children don't learn from their parents the old songs, which are therefore forgotten. Some 'sinful' souls naturally are still joiking, and a certain number of the young joik when they are out with the reindeer. The most genuine of them have difficulty avoiding this form of expression of what they see and feel. But the lives of the Sami and their language are made poorer by the fact that they've been robbed of this part of their culture."

Demant Hatt would be glad to know that the joik never died out completely but was preserved within Sami communities and homes and by folklore collectors on wax cylinders and audiotape, thus allowing later generations to hear their ancestors joiking. The joik in its many guises is an integral part of the Sami music scene and has evolved in modern times to include young artists who both rap and joik.—Trans.]

"The Fox Tricks the Bear and Makes a Sami Man Rich"
The first part of this story is well known among the northern Sami people and has already been recorded by J. A. Friis. It was particularly

alive in the consciousness of the Sami when I lived in Torne Lapmark [among the Talma Sami at Lake Torneträsk] in 1907. If something was too hot, one said with a smile, "Bakas, bakas, rieban-galles!" ["Hot, hot, old fox!"]. The second half of the story about how the fox made the Sami man rich is not told here. We recorded it first, along with the previous one, in 1916, among the Karesuando Sami, where it was told to us by a Sami girl from Kautokeino. [The name "Elle Ristine" or "Elli Ristina" was a common one in Sami families. But there is a possibility that the narrator was Anni Rasti's sister, Elle Ristine Nutti, whom the Hatts and Rastis visited on the island of Kvaløya the summer of 1916.]

The image depicts the moment when the fire flares up from the pit and burns the tied-up bear, who in his anguish calls to the fox, "Hot, hot, old fox!"

Folktales

"Njavisjædne and Atsisjædne"

[I have divided the original long narrative, made up of two sections with different plots and motifs, into two separate stories. In the second story, "The Daughters of Njavisjædne and Atsisjædne," there are several supernatural characters: a merman, an old Halde woman, and a *draugen*. This *draugar*, called here a sea-monster, is a word from Old Norse referring to a revenant or corpse that has come alive again. *Draugar*, especially sea-*draugar*, are frequent in Northern Norwegian folktales but less common in Sami tales.—Trans.]

We have many variants of this tale from the Kautokeino, Karesuando, and Torne [Talma] Sami. Atsisjædne always appears as an evil woman, most often an unjust stepmother, but the [expected] punishment for her misdeeds never takes place. She is burned to death and transformed into a beetle. The Sami call this little carrion beetle (Silpha lapponica) *hætsjelin* or *atsisjædne*, and it should always be thrown into the flames when it shows up around the fire circle. It calls out: "Don't burn my small breasts!" The same evil woman is said to have been fond of finery, and since the little black beetle appears to have a white "kerchief around the neck," one says of a girl who is wearing a light-colored kerchief that she is "fine as a *hætsjelin.*"

The witches' broom on birch trees is what the Sami call the *hætsjelin's* bundle of reins. [Witches' broom is a deformity in a tree, where a dense mass of shoots grows from a single point, sometimes caused by pathogens.–Trans.]

Tales of Atsisjædne and Njavisjædne are in J. A. Friis, *Lappish Mythology, Folktales, and Legends* [1871] and in Qvigstad and Sandberg, *Lappish Folktales and Legends* [1887]. They largely resemble those published here, though in a collection of Sami folklore one can't leave out tales of Atsisjædne, Stallo, and the Chudes, even if these stories resemble those recorded earlier.

I will add here a couple of stepmother variants from the Karesuando Sami. [One of these is written in the 1916 field notebooks, as told by Anni Rasti.–Trans.]

Atsisjædne married a widower, and they each had a grown daughter. Atsisjædne treated her stepdaughter badly, making her go hungry and work hard. To be completely rid of her, Atsisjædne set the girl to spinning at the edge of a gorge, at the bottom of which there was a deep spring. The ball of yarn rolled away from the girl, and when she tried to snatch it, she fell into the spring. But down there she met the good Haldes (the spring's protector spirits). The girl helped them feed and tend to their cows, and she was useful at all kinds of work.

After a week had gone by, the Haldes gave her gold and silver and helped her back up to earth. She walked home, and as she arrived the stepmother heard the dog barking, loud and friendly: "*Viv, viv,* now gold and silver are coming to the farm!" Her stepmother grew envious seeing the girl's treasure, and she sent her own daughter down to the Haldes, but the girl was unfit for work and ruined the Haldes' cattle. After a week had gone by the Haldes sent her home but gave her fire and stones to take with her. The dog barked, "Now fire and stones are coming to the farm!"

Atsisjædne now sent her stepdaughter out into the wilderness, far away into the wild forest, so that the Evil One could eat her. But the small birds sang so beautifully for her, and all the animals were good to her. Eventually a fine gentleman came and married her, and they set off for his estate. Now Atsisjædne sent her daughter to the wild forest, but the girl struck out at the birds and scolded the animals, and no fine gentleman turned up to marry her. Instead, an ogre ate her—and the whole farm burned from the fire the girl had brought back.

Another Atsisjædne also had a stepdaughter whom she mistreated. She made her go around in tatters, while her own daughter wore finery to church every Sunday. The stepdaughter wept and was miserable. The Halde couldn't bear to see her sorrow and finally asked the girl to come to her and gave the girl fine clothes. She bade the girl come to church the next Sunday. The clothes made the girl invisible to the stepmother and the girl's stepsister, but in the church was a fine gentleman, who immediately fell in love with the beautiful girl. He gave the girl engagement gifts and took the measure of one of her feet. When the girl came home, she returned the clothes to the Halde, who said, "Come here in the morning as soon as you're finished with your work in the stable." The next day the fine gentleman came, and he had a pair of pretty shoes with him that he tried on Atsisjædne's daughter; he believed in fact she was the right one. When the shoes didn't fit, Atsisjædne commanded her daughter to cut a chunk off her foot. Meanwhile, the stepdaughter had done as the Halde bade her. When she was finished in the stable, she went to the spring, and the Halde brought her the pretty clothes. When she went to the farm, the gentleman saw immediately that she was the right one, and they went off together. The stepdaughter said, as the Halde had told her to: "My tears shall burn you up!" And thus the farm burned, along with Atsisjædne.

The first illustration to "Njavisjædne and Atsisjædne" shows the witch coming out of her tent door to call to her son, telling him he must not go over to the other side of the Holy Mountain, because she doesn't want him to meet his own mother. The son is on a hunting trip for wild reindeer and now stands on his skis downslope from the tent with his bow on his shoulder. Up by the tent is a drying rack full of meat, which suggests prosperity. The second image represents the poor woman's tent at the moment her son has slipped a piece of fat into the stewpot as he looks down from the smoke opening above, while the stepdaughter exclaims in wonder that there is fat in the soup.

"Atsisjædne Tars the Moon"
Karesuando Sami. The little beetle below the Atsisjædne stories is Silpha lapponica, *"hætsjelin,"* drawn by Johan Turi when he once wanted to show me how the beetle looked.

Stallo Stories

Stallo is one of the most vivid folktale figures of the Sami people; he is known everywhere, from north to south. One won't find a Sami, from the youngest to the eldest, who doesn't know stories about Stallo—or Stala, as he is called in the most southerly Lapmarks [Stállu in northern Sami—Trans.].

The Sami say that in the old days this evil old race lived up in the mountains, spread out here and there, living on their own, always wandering about, always ready to steal tame reindeer from the Sami, always lying in wait for adults and children—because the Stallo were also people eaters. If they couldn't find enough tame reindeer and people to satisfy their hunger, they went hunting for wild reindeer, bears, and other wild animals.

They never lived as a group together in a *siida*; they lived on their own, often unmarried. If Stallo was married, his wife was considered even more cruel and wizardly than Stallo. Her name was "Ludasj"—bedbug. In Pite Sápmi: "Rutagis." Stallo's dog is named "Hump" or "Rak." "Tse, Hump' hui!" Stallo shouts when he sets the dog on someone. Stallo's dog is also a sorcerer. If Stallo is fatally wounded the dog can lick him well again. That's why you should always kill the dog when you have killed his master. Stallo goes around whistling all the time so one can hear when he is in the vicinity. All whistling is taboo among the Sami: the sound of it is absolutely connected with the Evil One and with sorcery. I've often heard the Sami say when a farmer walks by the tent whistling under his breath, "That is a Datja (farmer). He's whistling."

The Stallos were very rich in gold and silver, and if a Sami was so fortunate to escape Stallo and to find his treasure, he would become wealthy for life. A portion of this "Stallo silver" is still found among one or another Sami families as inheritances from relative to relative. The silver has something of witchcraft about it. If you had received a "Stallonaste," the Stallo stars (a belt decoration with three heads on it), you could cure many illnesses with it.

The Stallos are dead and gone now, but they still have descendants. In several Sami families it's believed that they have Stallo blood. It sometimes happened that a Sami girl married a Stallo, or in a few instances a Sami man could marry a daughter of Stallo, and in that way Stallo blood was passed down. The Sami are mutually aware of who has Stallo ancestry, and this casts a shadow over those affected. I have heard a young Sami mother reproach her son for being "Stallotjivga," a Stallo boy. He was born out of wedlock, and she kept secret who the father was: he was not someone she had wanted to marry. It was only around me that she used the epithet, since she believed I couldn't know about such things, but by chance I had so much understanding that I could guess who the boy's father was.

Yes, the really dangerous Stallos are gone, but the Sami still fear them to some extent, and they are not quite certain if there might not be a Stallo or two up among the wildest mountains. I myself heard a Sami tell the story of having once gotten lost; to his joy he found an occupied tent and went inside. He didn't know the Sami people who lived there, and when he had been there a while and the large stewpot was set on the fire, he was overtaken by a sudden fear that this was a Stallo family he had come to, whereupon he quietly snuck out again, put on his skis, and escaped in great terror from the place.

In the Sami language, which is full of similes and comparisons, Stallo also lives on: deaf as Stallo, large as Stallo, thick or narrow legs like Stallo's legs. If someone eats alone, you eat alone like Stallo. If someone has too large a head, then it is as big as Stallo's head. This suggests that Stallo didn't have his head formed when he was an infant. And so Stallo's name lives on.

In Västerbotten the Sami told me that there is a place called "Stallograve." This was "some upright stones, over which Stallo had laid a large stone slab, like a memorial." From the description it must have been a grave from prehistory. And over toward the Norwegian border there is to be found a large circle of stones, which the Sami believe are the remains of Stallo tents.

Russian Chudes and Other Enemies

The Chudes [Čuđit in northern Sami—Trans.] are not like the fairy-tale figures of the Stallos: they are tangible enemies, bands of thieves, who cruelly murder and plunder. Judging from their names, Russetjuder or Garjelak (Karelians), these fearsome fiends come from the east.

While the Stallo tales are always told with a smile and a humorous expression, it's completely different with the Chude legends. A sense of helplessness and fear of a horrible and overbearing enemy that never shows compassion still remain behind these narratives. Long after the ancient Chudes ceased to exist, the name was passed on to other enemies of the Sami. In the tale "Tju'jaure," the lake is thought to have gotten its name from the Sami after the outrages perpetrated there; it has another name in Swedish, Ögonsjön [Lake of the Eyes—Trans.]. From the character of the tales, one might suspect it is not an ancient Chude legend, but rather the designation Chude is applied to the hostile Swedish neighbors.

"When the Sami Lived under the Earth"

Torne Sami [Lake Torneträsk area, probably the Talma Sami.—Trans.]

"The Sami Man Who Created a Storm"

[Demant Hatt identifies this story only as "told by an elderly Sami woman in Jämtland." The narrator was Märta Nilsson, and the story can be found in the manuscript "Long Ago."—Trans.]

"The Sami Girls Who Escaped the Bandits" (Jämtland)

[This story, told by Märta Nilsson, has been added from the manuscript "Long Ago."—Trans.]

"Nuelesgiete" (Härjedalen and Jämtland)

Judging from the previous legends, it appears that these southern Sami have been roughly treated by their former neighbors. Their territories have not been as large and inaccessible as those of their northern kinsfolk. The invincible race hatred that is particularly powerfully developed among the farmers found it easier to strike its target. Until very recently the Sami have suffered harm from the property owners. The actions of the farm and mill owner [William] Farup in Härjedalen took place only a few decades back. When there has been such unrest so recently, when the Sami and reindeer had no rights, one can easily understand what relations might have been like further back in time, when there was little justice, especially for the "gray Lapp."

When a people live under stress in their surroundings and feel persecuted, it is not strange if they resort to a belief in supernatural protection. The southern Sami think of the northern Sami as possessing great gifts, weapons, and magical talents, and the Nuelesgiete must certainly be regarded as mighty kin, who protect the weaker and distressed. That the southern Sami are simultaneously frightened of those supernatural Sami from the north and ascribe to them horrible qualities has to do with the idea, known among other indigenous people, that what lies outside the normal horizon, what is unknown, has the shadow of the sinister. People and circumstances assume proportions that are too large, both good and evil. Different, unknown branches of the Sami are mutually frightened of each other. The Sami are in general quite strikingly frightened of other people, much more frightened than is commonly believed. In 1908 a commission was appointed for the investigation of the northern Sami's circumstances relative to the Norwegian desire to change the migration periods. Two Sami men from Västerbotten were in this commission. I met them later in Karesuando, and they related that they had been somewhat anxious about the journey to their northern Sami kin, especially since the older people in the family believed it could be dangerous because "up there in the north there are probably cannibals."

tales of ghosts and pestilent spirits, stories about murdered babies who come back to haunt their parents, and a number of legends that show the Sami as both persecuted by their enemies and cleverly resistant. *By the Fire* is also a work of graphic art, incorporating and transforming Demant Hatt's visual memories of Sápmi as well as the influences of Northern European Expressionists of the post–World War I years. The carefully designed book was her own conception, the art meant to complement the vivid oral storytelling repertoires of the Sami individuals whose work is the heart of the collection.

How *By the Fire* came to be shaped and published in 1922 is a story worth exploring, intersecting as it does with long-standing Sami oral traditions and with the sociopolitical situation of the Swedish Sami in the early twentieth century. As an adventurous woman who visited numerous Sami families in remote mountainous tracts and small hamlets along the border of Sweden and Norway, Demant Hatt was well placed to record a world in transition. Although she was largely a self-taught ethnographer, she developed many skills as an interviewer, translator, and expressive writer to add to her formal training as an artist. Through her husband, the cultural geographer Gudmund Hatt, and their circle of colleagues in the Nordic countries and eventually in North America, she was able to draw on academic expertise in the growing field of modern anthropology. Most importantly for her work as an ethnographer and eventual folktale collector, Demant Hatt spoke Northern Sami and was well connected within two different communities, the Talma and the Karesuando Sami.[1] Her field journals are thick with observations about daily life among the reindeer herders, and the folktales and legends are naturally embedded within those observations, family stories, and place descriptions. Such detailed field notes make it possible to identify not all but many of the narrators of the tales and legends, some of whose names also appear in published and unpublished manuscripts by Demant Hatt, along with details of their lives. From these sources, it's been possible to restore the narrators to their primary place in *By the Fire* and to give a sense of how the stories may have been told to Demant Hatt, perhaps one-on-one for archival purposes but more often in community as social performances.[2]

Sami Traditions of Storytelling

The Sami people have long occupied the north of Fennoscandia and the Kola Peninsula of Russia, and at one time their hunting and fishing territories extended far south of the Arctic Circle. Hunting reindeer eventually gave way to herding and to following the reindeer on their annual migrations from plateaus and river valleys to forestlands and high mountains. The Sami lived closely alongside the reindeer in nomadic tent communities called *siidas*. Some herders, the Mountain Sami, covered long distances on migration over the high ranges dividing Sweden and Norway to the Norwegian coast and back again. Other communities, the Forest Sami, lived along lakes and rivers, fishing, trapping, and tending smaller herds of reindeer, while along the coastlines the boat-building Sea Sami fished and hunted seals and whales.

Like all circumpolar indigenous people, the ancient Sami had rich traditions of myth connected with the northern world they lived in, dark half the year and light the other half. In Sami pre-Christian religion, the sky deities included Beavivi, the sun, and Mánnu, the moon. The gods of thunder and wind and vegetation were named and worshipped, along with a host of other gods and goddesses. The underworld too had its deities, including its powerful female ruler, Jábmiidáhkká. Myths accrued to the reindeer, the bear, and other animals; to landscapes and stone formations; and to the northern lights. For the Sami, the earth was alive and imbued with spirit; animals, trees, and even stones had recently been able to speak. Male and female shamans, the *noaidis*, acted as intermediaries between the world of the living and the unseen shadow world, where ghosts walked and the dead could sometimes be brought back to life. The *noaidis* had the ability to heal, often by falling into a trance state and traveling outside their bodies, and to divine the future, with the help of chanting and skin drums painted with symbols. The oral tradition encompassed stories, sayings, and joiks—vocalizations that express or embody a person or a place. As in other indigenous cultures, storytelling for the Sami was a means of imparting traditional wisdom, both practical and spiritual, and often a combination of the two. Much indigenous knowledge about weather, terrain, hunting, herding, and medicinal and spiritual remedies, as well as proper tent etiquette, was passed on through multiple generations.[3]

Over the centuries in Fennoscandia, beginning in medieval times, the Sami were driven farther north and inland by encroaching settlers and by rulers who encouraged colonization so as to claim the northern lands for the crowns of Sweden, Russia, or Danish-ruled Norway. Lutheran missionaries came in force in the seventeenth century to proselytize, to convert the Sami, and to build churches in Sápmi. The clergymen destroyed or stole the sacred drums and sometimes publicly burned the communities' shamans as witches. They also abetted the colonization of the traditional hunting and grazing lands by farmers from the south and east. Into the early nineteenth century there was still recognition from the crowns of different states that the Sami had legal standing and the right to migrate across borders with their reindeer, even though their territories were continually encroached upon. Yet as the twentieth century approached, the situation of the Sami had become more precarious. The herders lost reindeer pasturage and land rights, and their protests were crushed in a variety of ways from laws regulating herding to social discrimination and hate crimes. The borders between the Nordic states closed, forcing herders to choose countries and often to move their herds long distances in search of better grazing. At the same time, the industrialization of the north brought mining, damming, and logging, which destroyed native habitat, and agricultural use of the land for growing hay and raising goats and sheep set the herders and farmers against each other. Intermarriage, assimilation, and emigration to towns and cities or even abroad further reduced the number of Sami. Many Sami hid their backgrounds or stopped identifying as Sami, including a number of Norwegian, Swedish, and Finnish immigrants who settled in North America. Those Sami who continued to live a traditional life in their ancestral homelands of Sápmi were routinely discriminated against. By the early twentieth century, with the coming of the railways and tourists, the Sami communities were on the verge of greater disruption.[4]

Emilie Demant Hatt was originally one of those curious travelers when she arrived by train in 1904 on a holiday with her sister. She found what she believed was an intact nomadic society and only gradually began to understand the ways in which the *siidas* of the Talma and the Karesuando Sami, with whom she lived for many months in 1907–8, were under siege through new herding regulations. After having learned Northern Sami both formally from the Finno-Ugric scholar Vilhelm Thomsen at the University of Copenhagen and then experientially through speaking and translating, Demant Hatt began to delve deeper into Sami culture from 1910 through 1916. On her own and then with her husband, she spent six summers among different herding districts in Swedish Sápmi, many of them in mountainous regions along the Norwegian border. Her travels were funded in large part by the director of the Kiruna iron ore mine, Hjalmar Lundbohm, who also published the series "The Lapps and Their Land," which included titles written by Johan Turi and Demant Hatt.[5]

In her eventual published narrative, *With the Lapps in the High Mountains*, and in an unpublished manuscript, "Long Ago," about her summer 1910 stay with Nils and Märta Nilsson in their *siida* of Glen, as well as in the field journals (which run to around five hundred typed pages), Demant Hatt chronicled a world in transition. Although the ancient traditions of animal sacrifice, ritual worship, divinatory drums, shamanic healing, and spirit travel were not in evidence, such practices were remembered in stories told to Demant Hatt by her older informants, who had heard them from parents or grandparents, who in turn had

Emilie Demant Hatt, 1910. Photograph by Borg Mesch. From Yngve Åstrom,
Hjalmar Lundbohm *(Stockholm: LTs Förlag, 1965).*

heard them from older relatives. A multitude of domestic customs, healing methods, and legends lived on within the Sami families and *siidas* that Demant Hatt encountered during her active years of fieldwork in Sápmi, and she recorded them together with observations on reindeer herding, childhood games, courtship, marriage, and child raising. She documented punishing state regulations and discrimination against the reindeer herders that she both heard about and observed in her own interactions with Norwegians and Swedes. But among the domestic details and the political observations, Demant Hatt also recorded dozens of folktales and legends. Like other collectors in the Nordic countries, she was fascinated by the humor, the eeriness, and the poetry of the narratives. Yet Demant Hatt's relationships with her Sami teachers, her interest in women's lives, her anger at the persecutors of the Sami, and her sympathy for Sami rights may have also influenced how she listened to and recorded the stories. In some important ways she differed from the Nordic male folklorists of her time.

Traditions of Folktale Collecting in Sápmi

Narratives about the exotic inhabitants of the snowbound northern climes—wizards and pagan worshippers who wore furs, skied, and traveled by reindeer sled under the northern lights—had long intrigued readers in Great Britain and Western Europe. One of the books with the greatest imaginative influence was *Lapponia* by Johannes Schefferus. Originally published in Latin in 1673 and soon a bestseller in several languages, including English, the book contained text and illustrations that proved highly popular in shaping a picture of the Sami as heathens and sorcerers. The large engravings showed people bowing down at altars or beating on skin drums. Over the centuries such images and narratives of the Sami filtered down into books for children. The Swedish-speaking Finnish author Zacharis Topelius published a number of works from the 1860s onward for children that included Sami tales. One of his most

Sami herders depicted in Lapponia *by Johannes Schefferus, 1673. Courtesy of Getty Research Institute.*

enduring stories was "Sampo Lappelil," which Demant Hatt had read and loved as a child. But these tales for children were also accompanied in Finland and Scandinavia by darker stories of "Lapp wizards," who caused havoc to sailors and unwary folk, and of vengeful beggars, who plagued the people of the countryside. Such narratives can be found in most collections of Nordic folklore from the nineteenth and even twentieth centuries.[6]

In 1841, following in the footsteps of the Brothers Grimm in Germany, Peter Christen Asbjørnsen and Jørgen Moe published the first collection of Norwegian folktales, a slender book followed by increasingly longer editions. Several of the stories had explicit Sami characters; many had themes and mythic figures similar to those told in Sápmi, such as trolls (Stallos) and Huldras (Uldas). In 1871, likely inspired by Asbjørnsen and Moe, a Norwegian professor of Sami languages at the University of Oslo, J. A. Friis (1821–96), published *Lappish Mythology, Folktales, and Legends.* Friis, who had studied with the Finnish folklore scholar Lönnrot Elias and had traveled extensively in Northern Norway, gathered forty-eight stories together from published sources and informants. Friis's collection was the first attempt to collect a sampling of specific Sami folktales, and it was widely read across Scandinavia. However, it was *Lappish Folktales and Legends,* a four-volume work compiled by the Norwegian philologist and rector J. K. Qvigstad, that became the best-known source for Sami folktales in the twentieth century. Following on several earlier editions of Sami folktales collected by Qvigstad, with the help of other editors, *Lappish Folktales and Legends* appeared between 1927 and 1929 and included 675 stories in the original Sami, with Norwegian translations.[7]

Large as it was, Qvigstad's collection covered only Northern Norway. Most of the eighty-one informants were men, who were interviewed either by Qvigstad in Tromsø or by his Sami-speaking assistants. Only about a dozen of the contributors were women, not because women did not tell stories but because Qvigstad found it difficult to encounter them. His key female informant was a twenty-four-year-old woman from Kautokeino, Ellen Utsi, who contributed forty folktales. Although Qvigstad listed his informants at the end of each story, he did not supply biographical notes. As had Friis before him and others who followed, Qvigstad considered Sami folktales to be a collective expression of Sami culture, not individual performances belonging to storytellers with choice-driven repertoires. As folktales emerging from geographic districts and dialects, the narratives in *Lappish Folktales and Legends* could be studied for themes and distribution, categorized by type, and compared to Norwegian folktales, which were generally held to be the standard model from which the Sami tale borrowed motifs, plots, and Norwegian words.[8]

Even before Demant Hatt came to live with the Talma Sami in 1907, she was familiar with the general outlines of Sami myth and folklore. As part of her studies with Vilhelm Thomsen in Copenhagen she was assigned selected stories from Friis and Qvigstad in Northern Sami; she had also read their collections in Norwegian. The majority of the Sami she met around Lake Torneträsk in 1907 belonged to the Læstadian faith, a strict cult of Lutheranism. They shied away from anything that could be considered anti-Christian, though Demant Hatt still managed to hear a few good stories about the underground people and Stallo, which she recorded in letters and which later appeared in *With the Lapps*. Fortunately, her friend Johan Turi was an avid collector and teller of stories of all kinds, and although she did not see much of him the first year she was in Sápmi, that changed in the late summer of 1908 after she returned from the reindeer migration to Norway with the Karesuando Sami. She was offered a former miner's shack at Torneträsk Station, where both she and Turi worked for the next eight to ten weeks. Turi filled many notebooks that Demant Hatt would take back to Copenhagen to transcribe, translate, and edit into the bilingual Sami-Danish work *An Account of the Sámi (Muitalus sámiid birra)* (1910).[9]

The Northern Sami word *muitalus* chosen by Turi means "narrative" or "memory," and in the context of his writing, the term covers collective and individual knowledge about hunting, animal behavior, reindeer herding, medicine and healing, daily life in the tent, weather, and migration. *An Account of the Sámi* contains about a dozen folktales, while *Lappish Texts* (1918–19), a bilingual Sami-English book by Turi, holds about three times that many, along with some riddles and sayings, making Johan Turi perhaps the earliest published Sami collector of Sami folktales.[10]

Johan Turi was a great source of inspiration to Demant Hatt, but he was not the only source. As early as the spring of 1908, she left the Talma Sami to migrate with the Karesuando Sami and to live closely in a tent with Anni and Jouna Rasti and their young daughter. In 1910 she moved into a tent for six weeks with two Sami elders, Märta and Nils Nilsson, in the Sami village of Glen in South Sápmi. In 1911 she traveled alone for some weeks in the summer in Ume Sápmi (Västerbotten) with members of the Ran district. That same year she married Gudmund Hatt, a young graduate student in cultural geography at the University of Copenhagen,

Johan Turi, 1908. Photograph by Borg Mesch. Courtesy of Norwegian Folklore Archives, University of Oslo.

with whom she shared many interests. During 1912–14 Gudmund Hatt did research and worked on his dissertation, "Arctic Skin Clothing," and accompanied his wife on three substantial summer field trips to several areas of Sápmi, where they interviewed and lived with reindeer-herding families. The Hatts further pursued their interests in ethnography and folklore while spending a year in North America in 1914–15. They began in New York by studying at Columbia University with Franz Boas and his circle, while also doing research on skin clothing at the American Museum of Natural History; they then visited Washington, DC, Chicago, Ottawa, and Boston, where they met a number of prominent Americanist ethnographers, many of whom were also folklorists.

Inspired by these ethnographers and by their own interests in the Sami, the Hatts planned to write a full-length book about the many regions of Swedish Sápmi and the various *siidas* and their cultures and traditions. In 1916 they spent one last summer around Lake Torneträsk and in Tromsdalen, staying with the Turi family and Anni and Jouna Rasti, where they gathered artifacts and collected more information and folktales. But though Gudmund Hatt wrote several papers on the Sami and eventually released a significant monograph on reindeer husbandry and though Demant Hatt wrote and published *With the Lapps* and edited a second book by Johan Turi, *Lappish Texts* (translated into English by her husband), their "broader collection of folklore material" mentioned in Demant Hatt's Introduction was never realized. Gudmund Hatt's career took a different turn after he accepted a job at the National Museum of Denmark in 1919 registering Iron Age archeological sites and artifacts. He then coauthored a popular geography text in four volumes, and by the end of the 1920s he was a professor of cultural geography at the University of Copenhagen and also played a major role excavating and preserving Denmark's Iron Age field systems. By the 1930s he was lecturing and writing books about geopolitics.

Demant Hatt herself moved away from ethnographic fieldwork and back into the serious pursuit of an artistic career. Nevertheless, she retained her many field notebooks from 1912–16, and these, combined with her notes and letters from 1907–8 and 1910 in particular, held all the interviews and stories that she would later draw on for *By the Fire* in 1922. In the mid-1940s, encouraged by the director of the new Sami department of the Nordic Museum in Stockholm, Ernst Manker, Demant Hatt began writing a manuscript about her summer with Märta and Nils Nilsson, which she titled "Long Ago." She also, with an eye to donating her ethnographic research from Sápmi to the Nordic Museum, typed up hundreds of pages of notes from her field journals. These pages of field notes offer many insights into the backgrounds of her informants and storytellers, as well as into the places and the circumstances in which the stories were told.[11]

One Voice and Many Voices

In large part, the narratives Demant Hatt includes in *By the Fire* were originally taken down in Danish in small field notebooks. The storytellers themselves may in some cases have been speaking in the Northern Sami language. Others, particularly in the southern parts of Sápmi, would have been speaking Swedish or a mix of Swedish and Southern Sami or the Pite Sami language.[12] In places, Gudmund Hatt's handwriting also appears in the field journals. Demant Hatt explained that from 1912 Gudmund sometimes helped her record notes during their fieldwork, especially when Demant Hatt wanted to focus on listening and asking questions. If and when Gudmund wrote down any folktales, however, it would have been in his wife's Danish version, since he knew none of the Sami languages.

That Demant Hatt wrote her field journals in Danish, while speaking Sami or Swedish with her hosts and informants, lends a more uniform voice to the tales than they might have had otherwise. As readers of *With the Lapps* will know, Demant Hatt's voice is distinctive, by turns lyrical, slyly humorous, occasionally outraged, her text full of illuminating details about animals, people, and landscapes. Sometimes in *With the Lapps*, she quotes her Sami friends speaking in Northern Sami, with a translation following, clearly to show the tone of their comic take on a subject or their kind rebuke to her. Demant Hatt eventually spoke Northern Sami well, and she had an ear for nuance as well as a good understanding of context as time went by. We can assume, then, that the folktales she recorded in her field journals are probably more or less accurate representations of what was said. The tales and legends have the stripped-down style of traditional folktales, with little description of landscape or characterization. They begin and end abruptly; the actors usually have no names or apparent motivations; and the emphasis is on the action. Some are very short, merely sketches, while others are more complex, with two or more plots grafted onto each other.

In comparing the published text of *By the Fire* with the handwritten and typed tales and legends in the field journals, it's possible to see that in most cases the print version exactly replicates the version that Demant Hatt initially recorded. In some cases, for instance, in the 1912 field journals, fragments of a story appear several times over the course of a few weeks, told piecemeal by several narrators, until a more complete account is captured and reproduced for *By the Fire*. In most cases, however, Demant Hatt only records a story once. Sometimes in her notes to *By the Fire* she observes that there are other variations of the story in print, from J. A. Friis or J. K. Qvigstad. A large number of the stories that Demant Hatt published in *By the Fire* are to be found in her field journals, often embedded among ethnographic notations on subjects that may have to do with the folktales.

The field journals are an invaluable source in identifying the storyteller by name as well as in pinpointing a more exact location where the narrative was recorded. Like some collectors of the time, Demant Hatt was more likely to categorize the folktale by geographic location and theme than by the individual who told it. Fortunately, the field journals usually include biographical details about the tellers, some of whom the gregarious Demant Hatt encountered briefly but memorably and at least two of whom, Märta Nilsson and Anni Rasti, she considered dear friends. By identifying the storytellers here it's possible to acknowledge their narrative gifts as well as to investigate more closely some of the motifs in *By the Fire*. Some themes and subjects, particularly the stories about animals and the malevolent but slow-witted ogre Stallo, were widespread in Sápmi, while others, especially the legends, may show a strong connection to one place and real historical events. Not all the stories, of course, can be connected with a teller, particularly those listed as coming from Jämtland but also several from Karesuando. But the majority of stories in *By the Fire* have been reunited with their tellers via the field journals.

Over the course of her fieldwork, Demant Hatt managed to cover a good deal of territory in Swedish Sápmi, from the more assimilated regions of South Sápmi in Härjedalen and Jämtland to the more remote areas in the mountains of Västerbotten and Pite Sápmi. Those travels, in addition to her long stays in 1907–8 and 1916 with the Talma Sami in the Lake Torneträsk region in northern Sweden and in 1908 and 1916 with the Karesuando Sami, give her ethnography and folktale collecting an unusually broad scope. Although Demant Hatt only includes one story in *By the Fire* that comes from the Torneträsk area, possibly because she considered that Johan Turi's domain, she drew on her experiences with the Talma in all her work. The only region of Swedish Sápmi that Demant Hatt was unable to visit for lack of time was Lule Sápmi, which includes Jokkmokk and Kvikjokk. She also never traveled in the far northern Finnmark regions of Norway and Finland, though several narratives in *By the Fire* reference those places.

Thirteen named Sami storytellers contributed to *By the Fire*, and there may have been others who told a version of one of the tales or who are not identified in the field notes. Some narrators are represented by only one or two tales, others by a more extensive repertoire. All lived in Sweden, though some had been born in Norway or had gone there to work as herders for a time. Of the four major narrators, three are women

Emilie Demant Hatt and Siri Turi, Laimolahti, Sweden, 1907. Unknown photographer. Courtesy of Nordic Museum Archives, Stockholm.

with whom Demant Hatt spent significant amounts of time in distinct regions of Sápmi: Märta Nilsson in Glen, Jämtland, in 1910; Anni Rasti on migration from Karesuando to Norway in 1908 and in the summer camp of Tromsdalen, Norway, in 1916; and Margreta Bengtsson on migration in Pite Sápmi in 1914. The fourth major contributor of tales was Anders Larsson of Frostviken in northern Jämtland in 1913. All four were or had been nomadic reindeer herders—Mountain Sami rather than Forest Sami or Sea Sami. They had married within the herding *siidas*; they had grown up in herding families and had often been told their stories by grandparents or parents. Other tales and legends in *By the Fire*, many from the summers of 1912 and 1913 in Härjedalen, Jämtland, and Västerbotten in South Sápmi, were told to Demant Hatt by active and retired reindeer herders, one as young as thirty-five and others well over seventy. The South Sápmi storytellers also included women: Anna Sara and Elisabet Rensberg from Härjedalen; Marja Maria Nilsson from Ottfjället in Jämtland; and Lisbet Nilsdotter, a Sami elder living in Fjällgåarden, a home for aged Sami in Undersåker, Jämtland.

Demant Hatt's interest in women as storytellers was directly related to her early predilection for observing and recording the details of women's and children's lives. In part this was because, when she arrived among the Talma Sami at Laimolahti on Lake Torneträsk in 1907, many of the men were out with the herds and she spent her first weeks with Siri Turi and other adult women and their children in the tent community. But her interest in activities traditionally associated with women was long lived; as an early twentieth-century, independent adventurer and "New Woman" from Denmark, she understood from early on that women's lives in Sápmi were worth chronicling in depth. That the majority of the folktales and legends in *By the Fire* are told by women makes this volume significantly different from collections by, for instance, J. K. Qvigstad, who largely relied on Sami men as his narrators. While many of the narratives that the women storytellers shared with Demant Hatt are either widespread in Sápmi or gender neutral, others feature girls and women as heroines, include more women as characters, or offer a slight twist in the plot that brings out a female perspective.

Cunning Girls and Women: Märta Nilsson and Anni Rasti

As Demant Hatt describes her in "Long Ago," Märta Nilsson was a woman of seventy-one in 1910, respected by all in the Tåssåssen *siida* of Glen, located in Sweden's Ovik Mountains across the large lake, the Storsjön, from the city of Östersund. Märta had been born farther north, in the Føllinge Mountains of the Frostviken district, to Lisa Persson and Olof Mortensson, who moved south in search of better herding lands. Because her mother was small and in poor health (probably from frequent childbearing), Märta was fostered out to a Swedish farming family until she was nineteen, when she returned to nomadic life. Even though she spent some of her formative years away, Märta must have seen her parents and other elders in the *siida* often enough to absorb a variety of stories, joiks, and teachings about spirit and health. She was well known as a wise woman in her community, with a good deal of practical understanding of how to use her healing talents for the benefit of others.

Demant Hatt found Märta Nilsson to be a warm and insightful companion during the late summer of 1910, and she documented much of what the elder told her about medicine and healing, as well as the personal histories of Märta and her husband, Nils, their sayings, and their thoughts about the Swedish tourists and farmers who came by. But Märta was in particular a gifted teller of stories, and in "Long Ago" Demant Hatt recorded how and where the stories were told in the community of Glen:

> By the hearth at home the good storyteller is appreciated, as well as
> the clowning of various youths. "News" is accepted gratefully, but
> also the ancient stories are popular. They never fail to captivate,
> however often they're heard. So do the stories about certain people,

Märta and Nils Nilsson, Glen, Sweden, 1910. Photograph by Nils Thomasson. Courtesy of Jämtli Museum, Östersund, Sweden.

who always "get into trouble," from Stallo of past times to one's own unfortunate companions. In such a way legends are created. These grotesque events are an eternal source of laughter and immensely entertaining, when you sit around a steaming meat stew in secure, cozy well-being.[13]

In her 1943 unpublished manuscript based on the 1910 field notes, Demant Hatt noted, after a section that recounted a few tales and made mention of giants and Stallo, that Märta "told me much more, which I'm not including here, since I've already published them in *By the Fire* under 'Jämtland.'"[14] Although we know that several of the stories said to have come from "Jämtland" were told by Marja Marie Nilsson in Ottfjället and Lisbet Nilsdotter in Undersåker, the others may well have come from Märta Nilsson in Glen, including "Dangerous to Sleep by a Juniper Bush," with its advice for how to tempt a lizard out of your stomach. Märta Nilsson was, as Demant Hatt describes her in "Long Ago," a healer and wise in the ways of Sami medicine.

As an adolescent, Märta, like most reindeer-herding Sami girls, had often spent long hours alone in the mountains, including at night, guarding the herds against animal predators, particularly wolves and wolverines. "The Sami Girls Who Escaped the Bandits," taken from "Long Ago," illustrates a recurring theme in folktales told by Sami women: the threat that girls and women faced from non-Sami men and their ability to fight back or to outwit these attackers.[15] In this tale, a girl is out herding by herself when two bandits kidnap her and take her to their tent, intending to keep her overnight until the next morning, when they will force her to show them the way to the larger tent community. The two men place the girl between them as they ready themselves for sleep; each wraps one of her hair braids around his wrist, so that they will be alerted should she try to escape. But as the men sleep, the girl manages to pull free the knife from her belt and to hack off her braids. Too late, they awaken and pursue her; she leads them over a bog. Her light weight and knowledge of where to put her feet ensure that she doesn't fall, while the men slip in and drown. Another incident involving scissors is mentioned at the end of this tale, when a girl who is kidnapped while herding manages to stab her abductor in the eyes with the points of the scissors and blind him.

There is more than a hint of sexual danger in both stories, as well as a prescriptive note—*always carry sharp objects*—and the message that even adult men, however menacing, can be outfoxed. Folktales often have a component of guidance and warning, and a number of Scandinavian folktales also deal with the girls-in-peril motif, though these Swedish or Norwegian girls are generally shepherding goats or cows, not reindeer, in isolated mountain farms. While Märta grounds the first story as a legend from recent times, which happened "in the Harkel Mountains" to "Pål Fredriksson's mother, when she was young," the same tale is one of many about threatened shepherd girls that are also found in traditional Swedish folklore, under the category "Girl Held Fast By Her Braids."[16]

This theme of the resourceful girl who avoids harm appears in tales told by the Karesuando Sami (probably Anni Rasti) as well, for instance, in "The Sami Girls Who Stirred Up a Snowstorm," where two sisters use a bag of feathers to bring on weather that kills their abductors and allows them to escape back home with their reindeer. Young girls are also shown outwitting the fearsome Dog-Turks in a pair of stories told to Demant Hatt by Anni Rasti. In one tale, two girls are kidnapped by Russian Chudes who come ashore somewhere around Tromsø in Northern Norway and sell them to a Dog-Turk. By not eating the food offered, the cleverer of the two girls gets away and is eventually rescued and returned home. In another tale, a twelve-year-old girl is stolen by a Dog-Turk but manages to save herself and her brother. (Folktales about Dog-Turks turn up in several Nordic collections; they are also, according to the Swedish folklorist Bengt af Klintberg, widespread in European folklore: creatures with human bodies and the heads of dogs, who eat human flesh.)[17] Anni Rasti tells the tale from the young girl's point of view and gives her the pluck to protect herself.

Anni (Anna Maria) Rasti was born into a Karesuando herding family in 1866, the daughter of Nils Guttormson Hurri and Ella Maria Persdotter. Demant Hatt wrote in her field journal of 1916 that Anni's paternal grandfather, Guttorm Nilsson Hurri, was a *noaidi*; Anni's father, Nils Hurri, is cited as a source for several stories, including the warning tales about Dog-Turks. There may or may not have been a personal reason why Anni told stories of girls in peril. She herself had a child out of wedlock when she was twenty, a baby girl who was given an "emergency baptism" soon after her birth and called Agnete Annasdotter Hurri. The name of the child's father was not recorded. Until the early 1800s, girls who gave birth outside of marriage were punished severely by the authorities and the church. But to lessen the stigma, which had led in many cases to infanticide and legal charges of murder, the laws were eventually relaxed in the Nordic countries. Nevertheless, Anni had to be formally forgiven and "absolved from sin" by the church in 1887. Anni married Jouna Rasti six years later in 1893; he was twelve years older and doesn't appear to have been the father of her child; but he gave Agnete the Rasti surname, and Anni and Jouna had a daughter of their own.[18]

Anni Rasti was a talented storyteller and joiker. The first evidence came during the grueling migration of spring 1908 when Demant Hatt accompanied the Karesuando Sami over the mountains from Sweden to Norway. Members of the *siida*, including young mothers with infants and a number of children under the age of ten, battled snowstorms, snow fog, rain, hail, lack of forage for the reindeer, and melting ice bridges over roaring rivers as they struggled through the Swedish mountains. Anni held everyone spellbound inside the tent by the campfire as the storms raged outside, and a few years later, in *With the Lapps*, Demant Hatt offered a memorable picture of Anni (Gate, as she is called in the book) in full flood:

> Here they can still tell stories. Sometimes in the evening a group gathers, both young and old, in the tent. If Gate is in the mood, it's not long

Anni Rasti (far left) sits with unidentified members of her siida *on the spring migration to Norway, 1908. Photograph by Emilie Demant Hatt. Courtesy of Tromsø University Museum, Norway.*

before Stallo, the Underground Beings, ghosts, Dog-Turks, and more throng forward. Each one has something to recount and add, but Gate is one of the best of the storytellers; she smokes her pipe and with calm dignity expresses everything in a way that makes it alive and real. The listeners lie and sit around the fire and follow the narrative with deep interest and rapt attention, often interrupting to ask about details. It can be midnight before the thin tent door rattles after the last guest.[19]

In the summer of 1916, the Hatts returned to Sápmi for what would be the last time, visiting old friends around Lake Torneträsk in Sweden and then traveling by train and ship to Tromsø, Norway. They spent three weeks with Anni and Jouna Rasti in their reindeer encampment in Tromsdalen, outside Tromsø. Anni proved just as good a storyteller, and this time there was more leisure on warm summer days to listen to her folktales and to write them down. Most of the folktales listed as coming from "the Karesaundo Sami" were told by Anni Rasti, but a few came from her husband, Jouna. They were told to Demant Hatt either during the spring of 1908, when she accompanied the Sami herders from Karesuando on their long reindeer migration over the mountains to Tromsdalen, or during August and September 1916 in Tromsdalen. The Hatts also spent a few days that year on the island of Kvaløya near Tromsø with Anni's sister, Elle Ristine Nutti. According to Demant Hatt's field journal, Elle (born Hurri) was married to Nikolaus Nutti. The story attributed to Elli Ristina Nutti, "The Fox Tricks the Bear and Makes a Sami Man Rich," may have come from Anni Rasti's sister.[20]

In addition to the stories of young women outwitting bandits and Dog-Turks, Anni Rasti's repertoire included several more narratives about girls and women, both real and supernatural. "How the Sami Girl Tricked the Evil One" shows a young woman besting the Devil. "The Sami Lad Who Married a Halde Girl and Was Given Lucky Reindeer Along with Her" is a common narrative, told with many variations around Sápmi, about a girl from the otherworld who is tricked into remaining in the human realm and sharing her knowledge with men. Missing in Anni Rasti's version is the depiction of the girl as a temptress, which is more common in Norwegian tales, where the Halde (or Huldra in Norwegian) has a lovely face but a tail. Still, young Sami men who marry Halde girls generally fare better than young Sami women, who must fend off non-Sami men or creatures who want them for wives.

Anni Rasti's girls who stirred up a snowstorm were advised by their mother, a "woman wise in sorcery," or in Demant Hatt's Danish word, *troldkyndig. Kyndig* means "knowing," and like the English word "cunning" in its older sense of being wise (like the "cunning folk" of Britain who could heal and cast positive spells), the word as applied to girls and women carries an implication of female power. But, in fact, most of the daring that women protagonists exhibit in *By the Fire* has more to do with nerve than witchcraft—or with male fears of women as witches, which works to the women's advantage. In "The Blind Old Woman," from Västerbotten, an elderly woman stays behind when the others hear the bandits coming and flee. Her laughter has the effect of making the bandits think she's a witch and scaring them off so the Sami tent is undisturbed. Another Västerbotten tale, "The Russian Chudes Who Were Blown Up," features a resourceful older woman, the only one of the *siida* who hadn't run away, who calmly makes a stew for the enemies. While they're eating, she tosses gunpowder on the fire from outside the tent. She escapes but, quite satisfyingly, they are all blown to smithereens.

Dead Children: Margreta Bengtsson

Anni Rasti's tales demonstrate a great mastery of different motifs and genres, and she doubtless had more tales in her repertoire that Demant Hatt did not record. The Sami woman storyteller who is the next richest source for folktales in *By the Fire* was Margreta Bengtsson, whose eleven tales were all first recorded in Demant Hatt's journals from 1914 in Pite Sápmi. Margreta was born in 1865 to Nils Larsson Snuonk and Lotta Enarsdotter, nomadic reindeer herders who lived in a *siida* by Mavas Lake in the high mountains of Sweden, near the Norwegian border. When Margreta was five, she and her uncle were in a boat rowed by her father that overturned on the lake. Her father drowned, but Margreta managed to float on a rucksack of tanned reindeer skin to shore. Her uncle Per Persson Ruong also survived. He was a widower who had been married to Margreta's mother's sister. After Margreta's father drowned, her uncle married Lotta Snuonk and became Margreta's stepfather.

At age twenty-one, Margreta married Lars Bengtsson, a herder sixteen years older. He had been married twice before; both wives had died

Margreta Bengtsson, Pite Sápmi, 1914. Photograph by Emilie Demant Hatt.
Courtesy of Nordic Museum Archives, Stockholm.

in childbirth. Margreta, fifty-one when Demant Hatt met her, had borne five living children and had lost others to sickness, either in early childhood or soon after birth. Some babies lived only a few hours. It's possible that these births, where the child might not have been baptized, were not recorded, for Demant Hatt says Margreta Bengtsson lost seven children, while her descendants list three who died.[21]

The Hatts spent around three weeks with Lars and Margreta Bengtsson and their two younger children in the mountains, and while Gudmund was out helping with the herding, Emilie and Margreta often stayed behind in the tent, talking. Demant Hatt filled many of her small field journals with Bengtsson's information, including folktales about animals and Stallos. It's very possible that her repertoire was augmented by stories from Abraham Johansson, a traveling teacher, or *kateket*, who was born in Norway but moved to Sweden with his sister, Sara, also a teacher. As *katekets*, the siblings moved from *siida* to *siida*, teaching adults and children how to read and write and in the process picking up stories and other useful information and then relaying them to people in the next *siida*. Both Abraham and Sara Johansson (later Ruong) were at different times teachers to the Bengtsson family.[22]

Few folktales belong solely to one person, though some narrators tell them better than others. Like Anni Rasti, Margreta Bengtsson was a gifted performer. In 1953, when Margreta was eighty-eight, philologist Israel Ruong, the son of Sara Johansson Ruong, recorded her speaking and joiking on audio tape, in part to capture the Pite Sami language, which was even then in the process of dying out. Although her speaking voice sounds elderly, when she begins to tell a story or joik, it recovers amazing force.[23] No wonder Demant Hatt found Bengtsson such a wonderful storyteller. One of the stories Bengtsson told, "The Dead Child Who Came to Life Again," seems to be fully her own, longer and more developed than some of the tales of *eppers*, "dead child beings," that appear in other collections and that were widespread in northern Fennoscandia, particularly Sweden and Norway. Recorded mentions of this motif go

Margreta Bengtsson (far left) and her family, Saltdal, Norway, 1907.
Photograph by Captain Widerøe. Courtesy of Norwegian Mapping Authority.

back to at least 1673, in *Laponia* by Johannes Schefferus. In 1767 Knud Leem describes the *epper* as a ghost that exists "in a certain place where a child who had no name had been killed. They said that the ghost cried sorrowfully until it received a name and after that they could hear it no more."[24] The *epper* stories were widespread among the Sami, but they also were told in other rural areas of Norway and Sweden, where the *epper* was called an *utkastning*, or outcast, or a *ypping*, from the Swedish word "to reveal."

These folktales about a restless baby ghost that cries out and disturbs people in the wilderness, that often cries for its mother and asks her for a name, and that eventually seeks revenge on the parent who suffocated or abandoned it are obviously connected with infanticide, a not uncommon practice. Before the adoption of Christianity, abandoning babies was socially condoned, either because the child was ill or deformed or because the mother could not care for an infant. After Christianity was adopted and with it the rite of baptism, the killing of a baptized child was considered murder and could be punished by death. This sometimes led to abandoning newborns without baptizing them. In the seventeenth and eighteenth centuries the concealed crime of infanticide increased, in part because of the strict laws and in part because the Lutheran Church so stigmatized illegitimacy. Only in the mid-nineteenth century was extreme punishment lifted to prevent child murder and were baptisms encouraged of children born outside wedlock. In Karesuando the fear that a child might die unbaptized was so great that some children were baptized *before* birth or immediately afterward if there was any danger.[25] This might have been the reason why the daughter of Anni Rasti was given an "emergency baptism."

Stories about *eppers* also appear in Friis and in Qvigstad. One of Qvigstad's informants, Ellen Utsi, contributed half a dozen *epper* tales to one of his volumes of *Lappish Tales and Legends*. Most of them are short and often repetitive. Bengtsson's tale "The Dead Child Who Came to Life Again," however, has a well-shaped and powerful structure, which begins with the unexplained mystery of why two young people decide to kill their newborn—as with most *epper* stories, no motivation is ever suggested. That the mother stuffs a pair of scissors into the dead child's mouth follows the pattern of a parent trying to make sure the crime can't be traced by loud cries. But that the mother realizes later that she really needs those scissors again adds a homely, if horrific touch. There are other details that gently tinge the story with some kindness, including the aunt who takes the vengeful baby in and bathes it in the same water as she's bathed her own child. The bath represents baptism, and the act is one of integrating the baby into the world of the living.

Folktales and Legends: Anni Rasti, Anders Larsson, and Anna Sara

As Demant Hatt makes clear in her Introduction to *By the Fire*, she is deliberately unconcerned with folktale typology and slotting stories into anything more than rough categories, some of which overlap. She also doesn't offer a clear distinction between folktales *(eventyr)* and legends *(sagn)*, though she does use both words. Many of her stories about animals were known all over Sápmi, and in her section of *By the Fire* titled "Folktales" we find subjects that are also familiar from Friis and Qvigstad, particularly stories of giants and Stallos or, in one instance, the story in fairy-tale manner of a king and a princess whose hand must be won in marriage by an enterprising younger son.

Such fairy tales were part of Sami storytelling and similar to those collected by the Norwegians Peter Christen Asbjørnsen and Jørgen Moe in the nineteenth century. However, in *By the Fire*, Demant Hatt is clearly drawn to folktales with a more traditional Sami background, such as those of the two sisters Njavisjædne and Atsisjædne, as told by Anni Rasti. The figure of Njavisjædne, connected with the sun, is meant to be generous and loving, while Atsisjædne, the daughter of the moon, is cruel and underhanded. The story told about them, of a good mother losing her son to a female enemy through dishonest means, is a powerful one, and Demant Hatt writes about the sisters more extensively in her notes, where she includes two long variants.

This section also has a large number of tales about Stallo, and these come from Demant Hatt's hosts and storytellers in many parts of Sápmi. They range from straightforward, often comic tales of how the violent but simple-minded Stallo was tricked into losing his prey or into falling off a cliff to longer and more sinister narratives of what happens when Stallo's daughters marry Sami men. "Stallo Eats His Grandchild," told by Margreta Bengtsson, is one variation on the cannibalistic amorality of Stallo; "The Sami Man Who Married a Stallo Girl," told by Anders Larsson in Frostviken, is another. We hear Larsson's voice directly in his opening to the story: "Here in our district we've never heard anything about Stallo marrying a Sami girl, yet there is a story that a young Sami man was wed to a daughter of Stallo."

Tales of Stallo, which Demant Hatt writes about at some length in her notes, clearly have to do with the supernatural, yet they are also rooted in folk legend, and some have to deal with the theme of exogamy— marrying or having relations outside the tribe. Interestingly, the Stallo daughters who wed Sami men end up, often after futilely trying to warn their husbands about the true nature of the women's fathers and mothers, leading an escape from the parents. In some Sami folktales Stallo and his wife, Rutagis, drown or are murdered by the daughter and son-in-law; in other tales the daughter chops off Stallo's fingers as he pursues her in her reindeer sled. Demant Hatt mentions that some Sami believe that Stallos still exist and have stories to prove that they encountered a Stallo or Stallo family by chance. It's also believed that some Sami families are descended from unions with Stallos. As Demant Hatt notes, "It sometimes happened that a Sami girl married a Stallo, or in a few instances a Sami man could also marry a daughter of Stallo, and in that way Stallo blood was passed down. The Sami are mutually aware of who is of Stallo ancestry, and this casts a shadow over those affected."

Thus do folktales and legends blur together. We can see this in other tales told by the previously mentioned Anders Larsson, who imparted to Demant Hatt at least seven narratives published in *By the Fire*. The Hatt couple met him in 1913 when they were in the Frostviken district in northern Jämtland. Larsson acted as a guide for them and also brought them home to the house he shared with his wife, Sigrid Jonsdotter Streuka, in Värjaren. They stayed with the couple for a week, working around the house in exchange for stories at night, and then traveled farther north with him, which might be why some of the stories attributed to Anders Larsson in the 1913 field notes are listed as coming from Frostviken and some from southern Västerbotten. Larsson was nicknamed Klokka Anda, literally, "Clever Anda." But in Swedish folktale tradition a *kloka gubbar* was better known as a wise old man, a healer,

or even a sorcerer.[26] It may be for that reason that Larsson had a repertoire of narratives about tales of spirits and the dead; he contributed a
short *epper* tale and "*Stainak* and the Sami Man Who Died," where Demant
Hatt again includes his commentary on the action.

Larsson was likely a talented performer, because several of his tales
are hauntingly retold, including "The Sami Man Who Wanted His Dead
Wife Back," with its echoes of Orpheus and Eurydice, and the darkly
humorous legends of the Black Death: "The Sickness Spirit That Arrived
on a Stick of Wood" and "The Sickness Spirits That Froze in the High
Mountains." Similar narratives of plagues and fevers are found in collections of Norwegian and Swedish folktales, where the sickness is often
personified by an old woman with a rake and a broom. Such tales, like
another from *By the Fire,* this one by Anna Sara from Härjedalen in 1912,
"The Sami Woman Who Saw Fever and Another Sickness Spirit," are
examples of what the Swedish folklorist C. W. von Sydow first named a
memorat, a tale of a supernatural experience that happened to the narrator or a friend or family member. They are more accurately legends
rather than folktales in that they are said to have been felt or seen or
heard by the one who tells the story, and they are often ghostly. Yet they
have a basis in history; the Black Death swept away entire village popu-
lations in Scandinavia in the fifteenth century. The memory of such
events lived on for generations.[27]

The stories of the Dog-Turks, semi-human beings that Anni Rasti suggests her father had actually encountered in Tromsø, also fit somewhere
between the category of folktale and legend. Although these stories deal
with threatening behavior by creatures with the heads of dogs, the spe-
cifics of the narratives suggest that, like Stallos, such beings once existed
in a time still remembered. For narratives that fit the definition of historical legends, we turn to the last section in *By the Fire,* "Russian Chudes
and Other Enemies," which begins with tales of incursions into Sápmi by
organized bandits, apparently from Russia or Karelia, many centuries
ago and moves through history to the near present to tales of Swedish

Anders Larsson, Frostviken, Sweden, 1913. Photograph by Emilie Demant Hatt. Courtesy of Nordic Museum Archives, Stockholm.

Anna Sara (far right), Härjedalen, Sweden, 1912. Photograph by Emilie Demant Hatt. Courtesy of Nordic Museum Archives, Stockholm.

farmers and clergymen who persecuted the Sami. Such narratives were notorious within certain regions of Sápmi and were told and retold by the descendants of those who had personally known the perpetrators, the survivors, or the resisters.

Enemies and Resistance: The Rastis, Jonas Persson, Elisabet Rensberg, and Lisbet Nilsdotter

Most collections of Sami folktales include a variety of enemies, both supernatural and legendary. The Sami have to fend off stupid giants and mischievous nature spirits, as well as the more evil-intentioned Stallos.

They also must outwit the Russian Chudes and the occasional Dog-Turk. Qvigstad, in particular, includes a number of narratives about the Chudes. Legends about these mysterious robbers who are said to have come from "the East" are told in many parts of northern Sápmi, from Finland and Finnmark in Norway to the northern coast of Norway. A common tale, "When the Sami Lived under the Earth," was told to Demant Hatt in the Lake Torneträsk area; it shows both the adaptive methods that the Sami had to undertake to avoid being robbed and massacred by the robbers and the cleverness with which they fought back. In several of the shorter tales—"The Blind Old Woman," "The Russian Chudes Who Were Blown Up," and "The Sami Girls Who Stirred Up a Snowstorm," the first two from Västerbotten and the third from Karesuando—the bandits are thoroughly and inventively outsmarted.

Some of the narratives about the Chudes in *By the Fire* were told to Demant Hatt in 1916 by Anni Rasti and her husband, Jouna. These legends are divided in terms of who murders whom: in "The Headland of the Murdered" and "The South Wind Bangs against Bird Mountain," it is the Sami who are wiped out; in "The Russian Chudes between the Lakes" and "The Dreadful Ravine" it is the Sami who outmaneuver and revenge themselves on the Chudes. But stories about the Chudes were also found in South Sápmi.

A story told by Jonas Persson of Härjedalen, "The Sami Man Who Tricked the Enemies and Saved the Farmers," where a local man forced to be a guide for a band of Chudes tricks them into following a burning torch over a cliff, is well known in Sápmi, along with many other similar tales about a "pathfinder." The celebrated 1987 Sami film *Pathfinder* draws on this particular legend, setting it around the year 1000 and making the hero a young boy. In many versions of this tale, the pathfinder is a boy or older woman, perhaps to illustrate that, in fighting back against evil outsiders, knowledge of the terrain and quick wits are more essential than physical strength. In *An Account of the Sámi*, Johan Turi tells two pathfinder tales, both featuring a female elder (one of them a *noaidi*) as the cunning trickster who sends the Chudes after burning birch bark in the dark, over a cliff or across a lake, where they drown.[28]

Historically, the Sami have often been described as a peaceful people, who have no word for war and who prefer to retreat into the mountains and use their way-finding skills to throw enemies off their tracks. Yet the legends Demant Hatt included in *By the Fire* show fierce self-defense and proactive aggression and perhaps are revenge fantasies on those who have long harmed the Sami people. Remarkably—considering the historically documented legal and extralegal persecution the Sami faced for many centuries in Fennoscandia—in most collections of nineteenth- and twentieth-century Nordic folktales they are most often presented as the aggressors, for instance, as malicious wizards who stir up storms or foul shamans who cast spells that bring disease and death.[29] None of these Nordic collections tell the narratives that Demant Hatt includes whose titles point to violence against the Sami by Scandinavian settlers, including "The Headland of the Murdered" and "When the Farmers Wanted to Stamp Out the Sami." Even in Qvigstad's comprehensive compilation, such legends about farmers are missing. The threats to the Sami in *Lappish Folktales and Legends* are many, but they generally come from supernatural beings or Russian bandits from long ago rather than from contemporary farmers and even evil pastors.

Legends of those who intimidated and murdered the Sami appear both in Norway and in Sweden. In Norway, beginning in the nineteenth century, farmers from more southern provinces were enticed to the north with offers of cheap or free land. Their new farms were built in valleys abutting the mountains and were often in the path of the migrating reindeer. As more farms were established in the valleys as well as on the islands off the northern coast, where the reindeer had traditionally spent the summer grazing on the lush grass, the nomads and settlers came into conflict. The Rasti family and their *siida* would have heard many tales of conflict, some of which had become legends, and would have experienced harassment by Norwegian farmers themselves.

In South Sápmi, the enemies described in the stories told to Demant Hatt were almost always Swedish landowners and farmers, sometimes aided and abetted by the clergy. Their aim was not kidnapping no-madic girls or stealing a few reindeer but outrightly destroying the reindeer herds and murdering Sami families, including children. The level of vicious hatred directed at the reindeer herders in such tales as "Tju'jaure" and "When the Farmers Wanted to Stamp Out the Sami" is shocking and meant to be shocking. Although some stories have a more positive outcome, with the Sami managing to outwit or even kill the farmers who want to exterminate them, several end only in mass car-nage. Most of these narratives were collected by Demant Hatt during the summer and fall of 1912. During that field trip, Emilie and her hus-band traveled from the southernmost part of Swedish Sápmi, starting in the area of Idre in Dalarna, up through Funäsdalen and Mittådalen in Härjedalen, across the mountains of Jämtland, and through the Sami settlement of Ottfjället and the town of Undersåker, which was on the train line from Trondheim to Östersund.

In many cases we find variations or fragments of the same legend in Demant Hatt's field journals, as told to her by several people in dif-ferent locales. Quite often, particular villages are mentioned in the leg-ends: Ljungdalen, Mittadålen, and Undersåker. One story in particular, "Tju'jaure," bears closer examination, because some aspects of it align with a well-known reindeer massacre in Ljusnedal in 1891, just twenty years before the Hatts visited this area near Funäsdalen in Härjedalen.

There had been copper and iron ore mining around Ljusnedal since the seventeenth century, and the village, with a church and houses, was the site of a sawmill on the Ljusne River and a farm when William Farup, a Norwegian-born engineer, moved there and became the sole owner of what was called Ljusnedal Works. Eventually he became the largest pri-vate landowner in Sweden, benefiting from a decision by the Swedish government to offer lands for sale in what had been Sami territory, on which the Sami had paid taxes and been able to use the resources and sell them to farmers. The relatively low prices for such newly available agricultural lands may have been part of Farup's switch from light industry to animal husbandry, and he began to raise cattle and built a large dairy. Even though the Sami still had the legal right, as well as the "customary right," to graze their reindeer in winter in private fields, conflicts soon arose between the Sami and the farmers. These conflicts were fanned by William Farup, who was elected to the Swedish parliament and used his political position to agitate against the Sami herders and their reindeer. Farup spoke of the Sami as a scourge and was quoted as saying, "Anyone who shoots reindeer is a friend of mine."[30]

Although the Swedish parliament affirmed in a reindeer law of 1886 that the Sami had the right to winter grazing, this did not put the issue to rest, and a period of violence against the herders and reindeer ensued, reaching its nadir in 1891, when at least 150 reindeer were found shot on the land belonging to Farup. In her notes to *By the Fire* Demant Hatt mentions Farup specifically, and his name appears in her field journals as well. Only after Farup's death in 1893 and the purchase of much of the land belonging to Ljusnedal Works by the Swedish state, to be used for grazing, did the situation calm, but the old fears as well as the anger did not die, and they found their way into legend.

Many of the Sami people Demant Hatt met in 1912 had a political understanding of their situation regarding the punishing border regulations and the appropriation of their land by the Swedish state. Some were activists for Sami rights. Two storytellers from Härjedalen stand out in particular: Jonas Persson and Elisabet Rensberg, both from the areas around Funäsdalen.

Persson, a married man of around thirty-five, acted as a guide for the Hatts for about two weeks in Härjedalen and then led them farther north. He was born in 1877 in Hotagen; his father was Norwegian, and he himself had, like many Sami, gone back and forth across the border as a herder. Significantly, in his youth he had worked as a reindeer herder for the influential Sami activist and herder Daniel Mortenson, who,

Jonas Persson, with Eva Olofsdotter, 1903. Photograph by Iver Olsen. Courtesy of Røros Museum, Norway.

although Swedish born, moved to Norway and helped organize the Sami reindeer herders in the southern Trøndelag region (including the cities of Trondheim and Røros). Among other activities, Mortenson edited and published an early Sami newspaper, *Waren Sardne,* in 1910–13 and 1922–27. The stories or partial stories that Jonas Persson told Demant Hatt all had to do with threats against the Sami from Chudes or farmers, and several are notable for their accounts of successful resistance. "The Sami Man Who Tricked the Enemies and Saved the Farmers," "How the Sami in the Hotag Mountains Killed the Enemies," and a version of "The Disguised Farmers" come from Persson. He also told Demant Hatt a partial account of the events in "Tju'jaure."

Of all the versions of "Tju'jaure," the most complete one was told by Elisabet Rensberg, a herder who in 1912 lived not far from Ljusnedal, in Rutfjället, with her husband, Morten. Rensberg also shared with Demant Hatt another account, "When the Farmers Wanted to Stamp Out the Sami," which seems to take place in her father's time, farther north in the valley of Ljungdalen, where the Sami were not able to defend themselves because of misplaced trust in the Swedish farmers. "The Disguised Farmers" as published in *By the Fire* came from Rensberg as well. At the height of the conflicts between the farmers and the herders, in 1886, when she was fifteen, her uncle had been shot in the wilderness and left there dead, so perhaps the story of the Sami family attacked for no reason by Swedes had special resonance. In the case of Elisabet Rensberg's uncle, no official investigation was ever made into his death, even though a doctor maintained that he had been murdered.[31]

Born to the herders Olof and Lisa Renander in 1871, Elisabet was taught to read and write by one of the itinerant teachers, or *katekets,* and as a young woman she made her way to Norway, where she worked as a servant for a reindeer herder. Like Anni Rasti, she had a child out of wedlock, at age twenty-two. The father was the son of her employer. They did not marry because of his involvement with another woman, and she returned to Sweden with her daughter, Stina. A few years later she wed widower Morten Rensberg and had a son, who died when he was four. Morten died in 1920, and from then until her death in 1958 Elisabet Rensberg managed the reindeer herd and remained active for many years on a local level in the Tännäs district, which was unusual for a woman in those days.

One of the lesser-known aspects of Sami history in the early twentieth century is the role of women in organizing among themselves in their districts and in contributing their voices and skills to two Sami congresses. Elisabet Rensberg would have known or heard of Elsa Laula (later Elsa Laula Renberg), the author of the influential pamphlet *Life or Death? Words of Truth about the Lappish Situation*, published in 1904. Laula Renberg was a powerful public speaker; she was born in Sweden and moved to Norway after she married to herd and raise six children. Before and after her marriage, Laula Renberg traveled around northern Norway and Sweden, making speeches and helping to organize Sami women's groups. She was one of the main organizers, with Daniel Mortenson, of the first Sami congress, which took place in Trondheim in 1917. The Swedish Sami held a second congress in Östersund in 1918, and it's known that Elisabet and Morten Rensberg attended it.

The legend "Karin Wildstar" was told to Demant Hatt by Elisabet Rensberg. The tale of a mother of three who takes her sled down to Stockholm to ask the king if he really has plans to destroy the Sami has echoes in a true story of Elsa Laula, who, with other Sami activists, petitioned the king of Sweden in 1904 on behalf of her people's rights and moved to Stockholm to study, make connections with feminist organizations, and cofound the first national Sami organization in Sweden. "Karin Wildstar," while carrying the flavor of a fairy tale, with a king to see the true nature of Karin and to right the wrong, still creates a female hero with agency.[32]

Vanja Torkelsson remembers her grandmother, Elisabet Rensberg, very well, and she remembers being told stories in her childhood by both her mother and her grandmother of the "murders of the Sami families

Elisabet Rensberg and her daughter, Stina, 1904. Photograph by Nils Keyland. Courtesy of Jämtli Museum, Östersund, Sweden.

Elisabet Rensberg (age eighty-three) and her granddaughter Vanja
Torkelsson, 1954. Photograph by Einar Montén. Courtesy of Jämtli Museum,
Östersund, Sweden.

that took place," as well as of the valiant Karin Wildstar. Torkelsson says
now, "As far as I know the stories were true. Those stories were sort of
fairy tales for me. I think my mother and grandmother wanted me never
to forget what happened."[33]

By including such legends, both those of persecution and those of
resistance by ordinary Sami men and often Sami women (young girls,
mothers, and elders), Demant Hatt emphasized her own belief that
the Sami were a robust people with a rich culture who defied the odds
against them, whether their tormentors were human or unearthly.
The last story in *By the Fire*, "Nuelesgiete" (placed as the closing tale deliberately, one suspects), speaks of how the Sami have survived under

protection from supernatural beings called the Nuelesgiete, who live mainly in North Sápmi but occasionally travel south to watch over the Sami there and to "revenge wrongs against the Sami." This tale was told by Lisbet Nilsdotter to Demant Hatt in Undersåker, where there was a home for Sami elders, Fjällgården, conceived of and run by the Women's Missionary Workers, which became a Sami gathering place and was visited many times by the Hatts during their monthlong stay in Undersåker in 1912.

In many of the folktales and legends collected by Demant Hatt during the early twentieth century when traditional Sami culture was in the midst of great transition, supernatural protective forces and the ordinary heroism of the Sami flow back and forth across the boundary of believability. Their tellers used their tales to entertain, amuse, give advice, keep historical memory alive, and continue affirming that they were an ancient people who would survive. Demant Hatt saw all this at the time, and her field journals bear ample witness to the way that the tales and legends were an essential part of the texture of talk in and out of the tent.

It was only later, around 1920, when Demant Hatt was back for good in Copenhagen, that she seemed to see the stories as something special and separate from the field notes and to find her visual imagination sparked by their imagery. Then she must have decided to put together *By the Fire* with her own linocut prints.

The Illustrations

The strong black-and-white linocuts illustrating *By the Fire* marked a new departure both for Demant Hatt as an artist and for depictions of the Sami in art. Demant Hatt, who had received a thorough but conventional art education privately and at the Women's Art School at the Royal Academy in Copenhagen, initially produced watercolors and oil paintings of city streets, country farmhouses, and lamp-lit domestic interiors of family members reading and writing letters. Most of her early watercolors and sketches of landscapes and figures in Sápmi are also realistic. She drew babies in cradles or in bathtubs inside the tents, women doing band weaving, and men carving wood and reindeer antlers. She also made ethnographic sketches of objects used by the Sami: harnesses, birch boxes, winter boots, knives, and kettles. In 1914 she contributed dozens of precisely rendered pen-and-ink images of Arctic clothing, including the tunics, hats, and boots of the Sami, to her husband's dissertation on Arctic skin clothing, later published in articles and a book. From 1907 through around 1918, creating visual art took a backseat to ethnographic fieldwork, to her literary collaboration with Johan Turi on *An Account of the Sámi* and *Lappish Texts,* and to her own writing.

In 1918, back in Copenhagen, she began painting seriously again and resumed her connections with other women artists and the Danish art scene. Demant Hatt in later years dated her transformation from realistic painter to Expressionist to 1924 when, visiting a gallery exhibit of modern Danish artists, she suddenly realized how she could paint and wanted to paint. Yet her graphic art in *By the Fire,* which she probably began working on around 1920, already shows the influence of the German Expressionists, like Ernst Heckel and Karl Rottluff-Schmidt, who reinvigorated the craft of woodcutting with striking, sometime violent imagery and bold, simplified lines. The art and literary journal *Der Stürm* was well known in Denmark before World War I, and many German Expressionist artists exhibited in Stockholm and Copenhagen during the war. Although woodcuts were more popular among the German Expressionists than linocuts, which were sometimes disparaged as too soft or gentle, working with linoleum grew in popularity, particularly in the book arts, in Scandinavia. In Denmark, women trained as artists but, often unable to sell their paintings to museums and otherwise excluded from artistic careers, sometimes worked as illustrators, using various techniques, including etchings, woodcuts, and linocuts.

One artist who might possibly have provided instruction for Demant Hatt as she explored the use of linocuts to illustrate the Sami folktales was Ebba Holm. Although somewhat younger, Holm also was a member of the women's art association, Kvindelige Kunsterenes Samfund, founded in 1916. She was represented, as was Demant Hatt, in the groundbreaking Women Artists' Retrospective Exhibition of 1920 in Copenhagen. In 1929 a Danish translation of *The Divine Comedy* was published with over a hundred of Holm's linocuts, on which she had worked for many years. Demant Hatt could have made the decision to use linocuts instead of woodcuts for any number of reasons, but the style she developed for the illustrations in *By the Fire* was definitely more influenced by the bold lines of the German Expressionists than the more elegant and restrained work of other women book artists working around her.

Although Expressionism never had a distinct manifesto, there are certain features common in Expressionist art of the first decades of the twentieth century. Figures and faces are more likely to be types rather than individuals, and these figures are often depicted in dynamic poses. Many modernists of the time were attracted to European folk art and to primitivism and were inspired by imagery from artifacts in ethnographic museums, as well as by carvings, prints, and art produced by native artists. Whether Demant Hatt was influenced by Sami art in terms of the illustrations to *By the Fire* is debatable. She knew two Sami artists: Johan Turi, whose pen-and-ink drawings of herders, reindeer, and villages were published in *An Account of the Sámi*, and Nils Nilsson Skum, another self-taught Sami artist who also drew and painted reindeer and figures against a background of mountains and valleys. But their work, while distinctive, was probably not the inspiration for the linocuts in Demant Hatt's collection. Her graphic work has something in common with the woodcuts of John Saivo, with their crisp and vigorous imagery of herders, reindeer, and mountain landscapes. Saivo was born in 1902 in the north of Norway and became the first Sami to study at the state art school in Oslo. Saivo was only beginning his education there in 1921 when Demant Hatt was producing her linocuts; it's possible that Saivo was influenced by the graphic art of *By the Fire*.

The folktales in *By the Fire* have compelling imagery, and Demant Hatt had many choices when it came to deciding which tales to illustrate. We can guess that some of those she selected ("The Sami Man Who Wanted His Dead Wife Back" and "The Dead Child Who Came to Life Again") particularly stirred her visual imagination, because she did two illustrations each for those tales. Some tales that she chose to illustrate are set in the present world, with folk art overtones (reindeer sleds, tents, dogs), and others are supernatural tales with eerie or grotesque representations of figures alive and dead (a devil with horns, a skeleton, a corpse). She likes action: a man raising an ax, a woman holding scissors, a Sami whipping up a storm. Many of the lines depicting the sky and mountains are short, decisive, flowing cuts, as are the flames under kettles and infant-sized bathtubs.

In her Introduction to *By the Fire*, Demant Hatt is modest about the illustrations, worrying that they may appear "outlandish, and almost incomprehensible to those who aren't familiar with life in the tent communities." She adds that her notes at the end of the book attempt to explain in words what the reader may not understand visually. There are many stories that she did not choose to illustrate; only a few contain images of a Stallo, and none, sadly, include an image of the Dog-Turks or Chudes. She also overlooks the legends of Sami girls kidnapped by bandits or the Sami folk triumphing over the Swedish farmers. Since more of the illustrations appear at the beginning of the book, it's possible that she ran out of time to create as many linocuts as she would have liked. By November 1922, just as *By the Fire* was being published, the Hatts were embarking on a yearlong archaeological trip to the Caribbean.

The larger illustrations are joined by a scattering of smaller boxed illustrations and in some cases a small, unframed object or animal, such as a goat head or a snake. A small picture of a beetle for one of the Atsisjædne stories was drawn by Johan Turi. Many of the illustrations are dark, the white lines of the figures almost hidden, adding to the mysterious, supernatural effect. At other times, the contrast is much

EMILIE DEMANT HATT

VED ILDEN

EVENTYR OG HISTORIER
FRA LAPLAND

J. H. SCHULTZ FORLAG A/S   A.-B. NORDISKA BOKHANDELN
KØBENHAVN   1922   STOCKHOLM

Cover of Ved ilden: Eventyr og historier fra Lapland, *published in Copenhagen in 1922.*

stronger: blinding white snow and darker figures, recalling the photographs Demant Hatt took, particularly from the two-month migration she made across the snowfields and mountains in 1908. In most cases the figures are part of the landscape, a visual style that Demant Hatt would later employ to great effect in her long series of color-rich paintings of Sápmi that she produced from 1935 through the 1940s.

A few of Demant Hatt's illustrations for the tales in By the Fire are charming, but the majority are, like the stories themselves, both riveting and unsettling. The figures of the nomadic men and women depicted do not resemble in the slightest the cheery, troll-like figures of the Sami people created by John Bauer, for instance, whose watercolor illustrations were enormously popular in Sweden in the early twentieth century. Bauer initially came to Sápmi in 1904, the same year as Demant Hatt's first visit. Along with other artists, he was commissioned to contribute paintings to a large book, Lapland, which appeared in 1908. The details of these paintings in National Romantic style, especially of Sami clothing and craft, made their way into the popular Swedish annual Among Gnomes and Trolls, as well as other folktale and fairy-tale collections. Nor do the illustrations in By the Fire resemble the often humorous sketches and watercolors that Swedish artist and amateur ethnographer Ossian Elgström used to illustrate various publications, including K. B. Wiklund's first and second Nomad Readers. The folktales at the end of the second Reader, published in 1921, the year before By the Fire came out, include many about Stallo, whom Elgström depicted as a rather stupid-faced and harmless giant. Demant Hatt sees the humor of Stallo, but she makes him more frightening, suggesting that she gives more credit to the courageous Sami individuals who trick and kill this cannibalistic ogre.[34]

Ved ilden: Eventyr og historier fra Lapland was printed in an edition of five hundred copies by the venerable Danish firm J. H. Schultz, in conjunction with Hjalmar Lundbohm's series in Sweden, "The Lapps and Their Land."[35] The book received positive reviews in the Danish press about the stories, judged to be exotic but often entertaining, and the illustrations, in which, as one newspaper critic wrote, "She has tried to imitate the Lapps' primitive fantasy."[36] Its impact among Nordic folklorists, however, was limited. As mentioned earlier, at one time Demant Hatt and her husband had planned to continue with their ethnographic research among the Sami and write a full-length book together, but from 1919 Gudmund Hatt's academic career went in a different direction. Demant Hatt turned mainly to visual art after 1924, though Sápmi remained a strong motif in her paintings. While she wrote the occasional article, *By the Fire* was her last book about the Sami. As an ethnographer and folklorist, she was largely forgotten after her death in 1958. Some of the narratives in *By the Fire* have been retold, for instance, in a children's anthology of South Sami folktales edited by Kirsti Birkeland.[37] Demant Hatt's name also crops up in passing in folkloric contexts, generally in connection with Johan Turi and the production of *An Account of the Sámi*, where she has been noted, variously, as his translator, editor, or collaborator.[38]

Emilie Demant Hatt's significant achievements are most often absent from academic histories of Nordic and Sami ethnography and serious folklore research. In fact, she was the first and for a long time the only Scandinavian anthropologist to record the lives of women and children, an interest reflected in the choice of tales for *By the Fire*. As a sympathetic observer and a partisan of the Sami traditional right to land and resources, Demant Hatt included folktales and legends that do not appear in most collections. Instead of depicting the Sami as evil wizards or simpletons, she shows them as a people unjustly maligned and mistreated, even murdered, simply because they stand in the way of the farmers. While some tales told by the Sami illustrate the difficulties a small indigenous population has had in standing up to colonization reinforced by state and local authorities, there are also counter-narratives. These tales of resistance through quick and clever action are just as important in demonstrating why the Sami not only have survived but have maintained their identity and culture for centuries. In her field notes, if not in the published collection, Demant Hatt gave biographical details of the storytellers and often the settings in which the folktales were recounted, an invaluable guide to identifying such narrators as Märta Nilsson, Anni and Jouna Rasti, Anders Larsson, Jonas Persson, Margreta Bengtsson, and Elisabet Rensberg, who lived all over Swedish Sápmi. The stories in *By the Fire* are the heritage of these nomadic herders to their descendants and a gift to us.

It seems high time for a new generation to encounter Emilie Demant Hatt and the narratives and illustrations of *By the Fire*, as well as the talented storytellers of Sápmi who shared with her their lively, humorous, eerie, and engrossing folktales and legends.

Notes

1. Swedish Sápmi is divided into fifty-one Sami districts, or *samebys*, where reindeer husbandry is practiced. Currently the *sameby* is both an economic association and a geographic region. Many *samebys* still have the traditional names they possessed in the early twentieth century; others have been changed. The Talma district lies around the area of Lake Torneträsk and Jukkasjärvi. The Karesuando district is the northernmost Sami district, bordering both Finland and Norway. It is now called the Könkämä district, but in *By the Fire* I use the historic name of Karesuando. Demant Hatt's relationships with the Talma and Karesuando Sami are described in her book *With the Lapps in the High Mountains: A Woman among the Sami, 1907–1908*, edited and translated by Barbara Sjoholm (Madison: University of Wisconsin Press, 2013), and will be explored further in this Afterword.

2. Much of the biographical information we have on the narrators comes from Demant Hatt's own field journals, held at the Nordic Museum Archives in Stockholm (EDH papers, B1 Manuscripts, boxes 3–5). Additionally, two of the women are described at greater length in two works by Demant Hatt: Anni Rasti in *With the Lapps in the High Mountains* (1913) and Märta Nilsson in the unpublished manuscript "Long Ago" ("For længe siden"), which Demant Hatt wrote in 1943 from her field notes of 1910. Both Rasti and Nilsson were obscure enough that their lives were not remembered, except in a few census details, beyond their lifetimes, while Margreta Bengtsson, a major character in Demant Hatt's 1914 field journals, was a more visible ethnographic informant for many years as a native speaker of Pite Sami. Several of her tales were collected by the Swedish ethnographer Edvin Brännström in the early 1930s in *Samiskt liv i äldre*

tid: Edvin Brännströms uppteckningar från Arvidsjaur och Arjeplog, edited by Ivan Eriksson (Uppsala, Sweden: Kungl. Gustav Adolfs Akademien för svensk folkkultur, 2017). Bengtsson was also interviewed and recorded on tape on several occasions by Israel Ruong, a Pite-speaking Sami professor of philology at Uppsala University (with a family connection to Bengtsson), from 1939 to 1953. The lives of Margreta Bengtsson and her husband, Lars, were also researched by their family descendants and published in 2014 as *Dulutj: Lars och Margreta Bengtssons dåtida renskötselliv* (Arjeplog, Sweden: ArjeTech, 2011), giving a more comprehensive look at her history and circumstances. Another woman, Elisabet Rensberg, whom Demant Hatt met briefly in Härjedalen in 1912, has recently been included in a joint biography in Swedish of three South Sápmi women, *Tre sydsamiska kvinnorporträtt*, edited by Ewa Ljungdahl (Östersund, Sweden: Gaaltije, 2017). A number of Demant Hatt's informants from her travels are also listed in her 1928 article on the sacred drum, "Offerforestillinger og erindringer om troldtrommen hos nulevende lapper," in *Festskrift til Rektor J. Qvigstad* (Tromsø, Norway: Tromsø University Museum, 1928).

3. In recent decades there has been a greater focus within Sami studies on indigenous epistemology, and works on Johan Turi's *An Account of the Sámi* have explored narrative as a means of sharing knowledge. See Thomas A. DuBois, "'The Same Nature as the Reindeer': Johan Turi's Portrayal of Sámi Knowledge," *Scandinavian Studies* 83, no. 4 (Winter 2011): 519–44.

4. Interested readers can learn more about the historical and political situation of the Sami, particularly in Swedish Sápmi in the early decades of the twentieth century, in Demant Hatt's travel narrative, *With the Lapps in the High Mountains*, and in my biography of Demant Hatt, *Black Fox: A Life of Emilie Demant Hatt, Artist and Ethnographer* (Madison: University of Wisconsin Press, 2017). For a general overview of Sami history and culture, see Veli-Pekka Lehtola, *The Sámi People: Traditions in Transition*, translated by Linna Weber Müller-Wille (Fairbanks: University of Alaska Press, 2004).

5. Lundbohm, for all his support of Demant Hatt and of Sami friends like Johan Turi, as well as his significant role as the publisher of books about Sápmi, played a controversial role in promoting the Swedish policy of "Lapps should remain Lapps" *(Lapp ska vara Lapp)*, that is, the policy of excluding the reindeer-herding Sami from education, work, and Scandinavian society, so that they could continue living a traditional but circumscribed and "protected" existence as herders.

6. See, for instance, tales about the Sami in *Scandinavian Folktales*, translated and edited by Jacqueline Simpson (New York: Penguin Books, 1988), who writes, "Being semi-nomadic outsiders, linguistically and culturally distinct from the main population, [the indigenous Sami, along with ethnic Finns and gypsies] were viewed with intense suspicion. Some tales show their magic being put to good use (against vermin,

in particular), but they were more often represented as dangerous and vindictive, and in popular imagination there is no hard and fast division between them and the wholly evil shape-changers and practitioners of witchcraft" (123).

7. Just Knud Qvigstad, *Lappiske eventyr og sagn* (Oslo: Aschehoug, 1927–29). An annotated edition of 309 tales, *Samiske beretninger*, edited by Brita Pollan, is available in Norwegian (Oslo: Aschehoug, 1997). A selection of tales from Qvigstad also appears in the original Northern Sami in the collection of myths, joiks, and stories in *Min njálmmálas árbevierru: Máidnasat, myhtat ja muitalusat*, edited by Harald Gaski, J. T. Solbakk, and A. Solbakk (Karasjok, Norway: Davvi Girji, 2004).

8. It has been possible to reconstruct the lives and experiences of many of the informants as well as the methods Qvigstad used to record and retell the stories. In her dissertation, "Revoicing Sámi Narratives: North Sámi Storytelling at the Turn of the Twentieth Century" (PhD diss., Umeå University, 2008), Coppélie Cocq takes a close look at volume 2 of *Lappish Folktales and Legends*, from Troms and Finnmark, and discusses the contributions—and silencing—of three of the storytellers: Ellen Utsi, Isak Eira, and Per Bær.

9. *Muitalus sámiid birra / En bog om lappernes liv* was first published in 1910, translated and edited by Emilie Demant Hatt (Stockholm: A.-B. Nordiska Bokhandeln, 1910), and then later published in several translations, including in English (from the Danish) as *Turi's Book of Lappland*, translated by E. Gee Nash (London: Jonathan Cape, 1931). It was retranslated from Northern Sami into English as *An Account of the Sámi* by Thomas A. DuBois (Chicago: Nordic Studies Press, 2011).

10. Johan Turi and Per Turi, *Lappish Texts*, with the cooperation of K. B. Wiklund, translated by Gudmund Hatt, edited, with preface and notes, by Emilie Demant Hatt (Copenhagen: Det Kongelige Danske Videnskabernes Selskab, 1918–19). The Sami-speaking Swedish-Sami pastor Lars Levi Læstadius wrote *Fragments of Lappish Mythology*, edited by Juha Pentikäinen, translated by Borje Vahamaki (Beaverton, Ontario: Aspasia Books, 2002), a collection of Sami mythology, religious beliefs, and folktales, between 1838 and 1845. It was commissioned for the French-led La Recherche Expedition of 1838–40 but was lost and not discovered for decades. It was not published in Swedish until 1997.

11. Emilie Demant Hatt, "For længe siden" ["Long Ago"], Nordic Museum Archives, Stockholm, EDH papers, B1 Manuscripts, box 4. Manuscript-length notes typed from field notebooks (1912, 1913, 1914, 1916), boxes 3–5.

12. Of the Sami languages still in use in Fennoscandia and Russia, Northern Sami, with some twenty thousand speakers, is most widely known (from around the Kiruna area of Sweden up through Northern Norway). Other Sami languages are Lule, Ume, Pite, Southern Sami, Inari, Skolt, and Kildin (Kemi, Akkala, and Ter Sami are considered extinct).

13. "Long Ago," 66.

14. Ibid., 72.

15. Ibid., 58–59.

16. Bengt af Klintberg, *The Types of the Swedish Folk Legend* (Helsinki: FF Communications, 2010), 439.

17. Bengt af Klintberg, *Svenska folksägner* (Stockholm: Norstedts, 1972), 10. Af Klintberg connects the tales to a folk myth associated with Charles XII and his wars, resulting in a debt to Turkey: the debt was to be paid by slaughtering Swedish orphans and sending them in barrels to Turkey.

18. See the section "The History of Punishments for Infanticide," in Juha Pentikäinen, *The Nordic Dead-Child Tradition. Nordic Dead-Child Beings: A Study in Comparative Religion* (Helsinki: Suomalainen Tiedeakatemia, 1968), 93–100. Census dates on the Rasti family and church records were kindly provided by Cuno Bernardsson at the University Library in Umeå, Sweden.

19. Demant Hatt, *With the Lapps*, 125.

20. The typed notes from 1916, which include the Hatts' visit to see the Rastis in Tromsdalen but don't continue with the rest of their trip, include notebooks numbered I through IV. The pages end at 101, just after one of the Atsisjævdne stories. It's possible that one of the notebooks went missing after *By the Fire* and that it might have included other tales listed as from the Karesuando Sami.

21. In her 1914 notes, Demant Hatt records nine children, seven of whom died. The Bengtsson family records eight births, three of whom died.

22. In 1914, the Russian-born ethnographer and writer Torsten Kolmodin published a slender book, *Folk Beliefs, Customs, and Legends from Pite Lapmark [Folktro, seder och sägner från Pite Lappmark]* (Stockholm: A.-B. Nordiska Bokhandeln, 1914), which included several stories attributed to A.J. or Abraham Johansson, and three of them—"The Bear That Carried Jesus over the River," "Stallo, Who Was Tricked," and "Stallo Eats His Grandchild"—are stories that Demant Hatt recorded from Margreta Bengtsson.

23. The recordings are available at the Institute for Language and Folklore in Uppsala, Sweden.

24. Knud Leem, *Beskrivelse over Finnmarkens Lapper* (1767), 426, as quoted in Pentikäinen, *The Nordic Dead-Child Tradition*, 299.

25. Pentikäinen, *The Nordic Dead-Child Tradition*, 302.

26. af Klintberg, *The Types of the Swedish Folk Legend*, 242.

27. Reimund Kvideland and Henning K. Sehmsdorf, eds., *Scandinavian Folk Belief and Legend* (Minneapolis: University of Minnesota Press, 1980), 19–20.

28. Turi, *An Account of the Sámi*, 148–52. See also Cocq's chapter 7, "Defensive Folk-

lore: The Enemy as Factor of Cohesion in Sámi Narratives," in *Revoicing Sami Narratives*. Thomas A. DuBois discusses pathfinders in "Folklore, Boundaries, and Audience in *The Pathfinder*," in *Sami Folkloristics*, edited by Juha Pentikäinen and Harald Gaski (NNF publications 6. Turku, Finland: NNF, Abo Akademi University, 2000).

29. This can be seen in collections translated into English, such as Simpson's *Scandinavian Folktales*; *Folktales of Norway*, edited by Reidar Thorwald Christiansen, translated by Pat Shaw Iversen (Chicago: University of Chicago Press, 1964); as well as Bengt af Klintberg's comprehensive *Svenska folksägner*, where he only includes material on the Swedish Sami from the generally negative point of view of the Swedish storytellers.

30. Land seizures and unjust treatment of the Sami in Härjedalen and Jämtland are discussed in Lennart Lundmark, *Stulet land* (Stockholm: Ordfront, 2017), chap. 14.

31. Vanja Torkelsson, personal communication, 2 January 2018.

32. For more on Elsa Laula Renberg, see Siri Broch Johansen, *Elsa Laula Renberg: Historien om samefolkets store Minerva* (Karasjok, Norway: ČálliidLágádus, 2015). More information on Sami political organizing in Sweden in the first half of the twentieth century can be found in Patrik Lantto, *Tiden börjar på nytt: En analys av samernas etnopolitiska mobilisering i Sverige, 1900–1950* (Umeå, Sweden: Department of Historical Studies, Umeå University, 2000).

33. Vanja Torkelsson, personal communication, 12 October 2017.

34. Over the years, the prolific Ossian Elgström tried a variety of styles in depicting Sami subjects, beginning in 1909 with his Jugendstil decorations and initial caps for *Solsönernas Saga* by Valdemar Lindholm. Ten years later Elgström was employed by the Nordic Museum to create a visual record of Sami clothing; his pen-and-watercolor illustrations to his own travel books *Lappalaiset* (1919) and *Hyperboreer* (1922) usually show Sami heads and faces or figures in isolation.

35. *By the Fire*'s publication was likely subsidized by Lundbohm, though the contract Demant Hatt signed was with Schultz. *By the Fire* was the last book published in Lundbohm's series of nine titles, which had begun in 1910 with the publication of *Muitalus sámiid birra*. In 1920 Lundbohm was unwillingly pensioned off by the mining company LKAB in Kiruna. He died in 1926.

36. K.F., "Lappernes Eventyr," *Berlingske tidende*, 17 March 1923.

37. Kirsti Birkeland, ed., *Staloer tror at månen er et bål: 25 sør-samiske eventyr* (Oslo: Cappelen, 1986). Demant Hatt is mentioned as the source for several stories.

38. See, for example, Brita Pollan's Introduction to Qvigstad's Sami folktales in *Samiske beretninger*, where Demant Hatt is described not as a folklorist and ethnographer but as a woman who was "deeply fascinated both by Sami culture and by the wolf hunter Johan Turi himself" (19).

Selected Bibliography

Cocq, Coppélie. "Revoicing Sámi Narratives: North Sámi Storytelling at the Turn of the Twentieth Century." PhD diss., Umeå University, Umeå, Sweden, 2008.

Demant Hatt, Emilie. "For længe siden" ["Long Ago"] and typed field journals, 1912–16. Unpublished manuscripts. Nordic Museum Archives, Stockholm, Sweden. EDH papers, B1 Manuscripts, boxes 1–4.

———. *Med lapperne i højfjeldet.* Stockholm: A.-B. Nordiska Bokhandeln, 1913.

———. "Offerforestillinger og erindringer om troldtrommen hos nulevende lapper." In *Festskrift til Rektor J. Qvigstad.* Tromsø, Norway: Tromsø University Museum, 1928.

———. *Ved ilden: Eventyr og historier fra Lapland.* Copenhagen: J. H. Schultz Forlag, 1922.

———. *With the Lapps in the High Mountains: A Woman among the Sami, 1907–1908.* Edited and translated by Barbara Sjoholm. Madison: University of Wisconsin Press, 2013.

DuBois, Thomas A. "Folklore, Boundaries, and Audience in *The Pathfinder.*" In *Sami Folkloristics,* edited by Juha Pentikäinen and Harald Gaski. NNF publications 6. Turku, Finland: NNF, Abo Akademi University, 2000.

———. "'The Same Nature as the Reindeer': Johan Turi's Portrayal of Sámi Knowledge." *Scandinavian Studies* 83, no. 4 (Winter 2011): 519–44.

Friis, J. A. *Lappisk Mythologi, Eventyr og Folkesagn.* Christiania [Oslo]: Alb. Cammermeyer, 1871.

Klintberg, Bengt af. *Svenska folksägner.* Stockholm: Norstedts, 1972.

———. *The Types of the Swedish Folk Legend.* Helsinki: FF Communications, 2010.

Kolmodin, Torsten. *Folktro, seder och sägner från Pite Lappmark.* Stockholm: A.-B. Nordiska Bokhandeln, 1914.

Koskimies, August V., and Toivo I. Itkonen. *Inari Sámi Folklore: Stories from*

Aanaar. Edited and translated by Tim Frandy. Madison: University of Wisconsin Press, 2018.

Lantto, Patrik. *Tiden börjar på nytt: En analys av samernas etnopolitiska mobilisering i Sverige 1900–1950*. Umeå, Sweden: Department of Historical Studies, Umeå University, 2000.

Læstadius, Lars Levi. *Fragments of Lappish Mythology*. Edited by Juha Pentikäinen. Translated by Borje Vahamaki. Beaverton, Ontario: Aspasia Books, 2002.

Lehtola, Veli-Pekka. *The Sámi People: Traditions in Transition*. Translated by Linna Weber Müller-Wille. Fairbanks: University of Alaska Press, 2004.

Lindgren, Lennart, ed. *Dulutj: Lars och Margreta Bengtssons dåtida renskötselliv*. Arjeplog, Sweden: ArjeTech, 2011.

Ljungdahl, Ewa, ed. *Tre sydsamiska kvinnoporträtt*. Östersund, Sweden: Gaaltje, 2017.

Lundmark, Lennart. *Stulet land*. Stockholm: Ordfront, 2017.

Pentikäinen, Juha. *The Nordic Dead-Child Tradition. Nordic Dead-Child Beings: A Study in Comparative Religion*. Helsinki: Suomalainen Tiedeakatemia, 1968.

Qvigstad, Just Knud. *Lappiske eventyr og sagn*. Oslo: Aschehoug, 1927–29.

Simpson, Jacqueline, ed. and trans. *Scandinavian Folktales*. New York: Penguin Books, 1988.

Sjoholm, Barbara. *Black Fox: A Life of Emilie Demant Hatt, Artist and Ethnographer*. Madison: University of Wisconsin Press, 2017.

Turi, Johan. *An Account of the Sámi*. Translated by Thomas A. DuBois. Chicago: Nordic Studies Press, 2011.

——. *Muittalus samid birra / En bog om lappernes liv*. Translated, edited, and with an Introduction by Emilie Demant. Stockholm: A.-B. Nordiska Bokhandeln, 1910.

Turi, Johan, and Per Turi. *Lappish Texts*. With the cooperation of K. B. Wiklund. Translated by Gudmund Hatt. Edited, with Preface and Notes, by Emilie Demant Hatt. Copenhagen: Det Kongelige Danske Videnskabernes Selskab, 1918–19.

Wiklund, K. B. *Nomad skolans läsebok II*. Uppsala: Almqvist & Wiksells boktryckeri, 1921.

Emilie Demant Hatt (1873–1958) was a Danish artist and ethnographer specializing in studies of the Sami reindeer herders in northern Sweden and Norway. She lived among Sami families in 1907 and 1908 and returned most summers from 1910 to 1916. Her two published books about the Sami were the travel narrative *With the Lapps in the High Mountains* (1913) and *By the Fire* (1922). Her literary collaboration with Sami artist and writer Johan Turi resulted in two classic texts, *An Account of the Sámi* (1910) and *Lappish Texts* (1918). She was an accomplished painter recognized in Denmark and Sweden for her Expressionist landscapes of Sápmi, fifty of which are owned by the Nordic Museum in Stockholm.

Barbara Sjoholm is the author of *Black Fox: A Life of Emilie Demant Hatt, Artist and Ethnographer* and the editor and translator of Emilie Demant Hatt's narrative *With the Lapps in the High Mountains*. Her many books include *The Palace of the Snow Queen: Winter Travels in Lapland* and a novel about Demant Hatt's youth, *Fossil Island*. Her translations from Norwegian and Danish have received awards and fellowships from the American-Scandinavian Foundation and the National Endowment for the Arts.